perfect
greek

This is a Parragon Publishing book
First published in 2006

Parragon Publishing
Queen Street House
4 Queen Street
Bath BA1 1HE, UK

ISBN 1-40548-858-1

Printed in China

This book uses imperial, metric, and US cup measurements. Follow the same units of measurement throughout; do not mix imperial and metric. All spoon measurements are level, unless otherwise stated: teaspoons are assumed to be 5ml, and tablespoons are assumed to be 15ml. Unless otherwise stated, milk is assumed to be whole, eggs and individual fruits such as bananas are medium, and pepper is freshly ground black pepper.

Recipes using raw or very lightly cooked eggs should be avoided by infants, the elderly, pregnant women, convalescents, and anyone suffering from an illness. Pregnant and breast-feeding women are advised to avoid eating peanuts and peanut products.

perfect

greek

introduction

The cuisine of Greece is a reflection of this wonderful country of sapphire skies and turquoise seas, pretty whitewashed houses, terraced olive groves with their curiously twisted trees, and, above all, of warm, generous, hospitable people. The country's culinary tradition is as long as its history and much of the food that is eaten today, especially on the smaller, unspoilt islands where a simple lifestyle is still followed, probably does not differ greatly from that enjoyed by the ancient Greeks around 2,500 years ago.

A Greek meal is a leisurely, sociable affair, often taken in the open air. The diet is based on a predominance of vegetables and

salads, grilled fresh fish and meat, fruit, and yogurt, all flavored and seasoned with olive oil, lemons, wine, and fragrant herbs such as thyme and oregano, which grow wild on the hillsides and are used in abundance.

A typical meal starts with a mezze, followed by a main course served with salad and crusty, freshly baked bread. Vegetables are usually served after the main course rather than with it, and the meal ends with fresh fruit, a dessert, or ice cream.

The emphasis is very much on the use of fresh, seasonal produce. Seafood is caught and brought in to the markets daily, sheep and goats are reared to provide meat and milk, pigs are also bred for their meat, and chickens are kept for both meat and eggs. A range of vegetables—eggplants, zucchini, bell peppers, onions, garlic, and tomatoes—is locally grown and found in every Greek kitchen, together with a few staples such as cheese, honey, canned

tuna and sardines, salted capers, olives, and of course olive oil.

Greek ingredients are now readily available in other countries, so if you are an epicure—the Greek word for a lover of good food—get cooking today!

Good health!

mezzes & soups

The Greek "mezze" is a wonderful reflection of the country and its way of life—an irresistible collection of dips, deep-fried seafood, stuffed vine leaves, pastries, tiny sausages, olives, and nuts, pleasing both to the eye and to the tastebuds, to be consumed at a relaxed and leisurely pace. If the mezze can be enjoyed out in the open air beneath a cloudless blue sky, the scene will be set to perfection.

Greek dips have become famous far beyond the boundaries of the country, perhaps the most familiar being the smoked cod roe dip, taramasalata, the chickpea and sesame dip, hummus, and the garlicky yogurt and cucumber dip, tzatziki, which also works as a delicious chilled soup with the addition of chicken stock. Soups are popular in Greece, particularly the classic *soúpa avgolémono*, a simple consommé thickened and flavored with an egg and lemon sauce, and the filling and satisfying fishermen's soup, traditionally made with the catch of the day.

The mezze is always served with bread, often the soft, flat pita bread that is ideal for scooping up dips or stuffing with sausages and salad, and accompanied with a glass of beer, wine, or the distinctive aniseed-flavored apéritif, ouzo, which you either hate—or absolutely love!

smoked cod roe dip

ingredients

SERVES 6

8 oz/225 g smoked cod roe or
    fresh gray mullet roe
1 small onion, quartered
2 oz/55 g/$\frac{1}{4}$ cup fresh white
    bread crumbs
1 large garlic clove, crushed
grated rind and juice of
    1 large lemon
5 fl oz/150 ml/$\frac{1}{3}$ cup extra-
    virgin olive oil
6 tbsp hot water
pepper
black Greek olives, capers,
    and chopped flat-leaf
    parsley, to garnish
crackers, potato chips, or pita
    bread, to serve

method

1 Remove the skin from the fish roe. Put the onion in a food processor and chop finely. Add the cod roe in small pieces and blend until smooth. Add the bread crumbs, garlic, and lemon rind and juice, and mix well together.

2 With the machine running, very slowly pour in the oil. When all the oil has been incorporated, blend in the water. Season with pepper.

3 Pour the mixture into a serving bowl and chill in the refrigerator for at least 1 hour before serving.

4 Serve garnished with olives, capers, and chopped parsley and accompany with crackers, chips, or pita bread.

smoked red bell pepper dip

ingredients

SERVES 6

4 large smoked red bell
peppers and juice from
the jar

3$\frac{1}{2}$ oz/100 g/$\frac{1}{2}$ cup full-fat
cream cheese

$\frac{1}{2}$ tsp lemon juice

salt and pepper

warm pita bread, to serve

method

1 Chop the bell peppers very finely and put in a bowl. Add the cheese, 1 tablespoon of juice from the jar of bell peppers, the lemon juice, salt, and pepper and stir gently together until mixed.

2 Chill in the refrigerator for at least 1 hour before serving.

3 To serve, stir the mixture and transfer to a serving bowl. Accompany with warm pita bread.

chickpea & sesame dip

ingredients

SERVES 8

8 oz/225 g/1^1/$_3$ cups dried
  chickpeas, covered with
  water and soaked
  overnight
juice of 2 large lemons
5 fl oz/150 ml/^{2}/$_3$ cup tahini
  paste
2 garlic cloves, crushed
4 tbsp extra-virgin olive oil
small pinch of ground cumin
salt and pepper
1 tsp paprika
chopped flat-leaf parsley,
  to garnish
pita bread, to serve

method

1 Drain the chickpeas, put in a pan, and cover with cold water. Bring to a boil then simmer for about 2 hours, until very tender.

2 Drain the chickpeas, reserving a little of the liquid, and put in a food processor, reserving a few to garnish. Blend the chickpeas until smooth, gradually adding the lemon juice and enough reserved liquid to form a smooth, thick purée.

3 Add the tahini paste, garlic, 3 tablespoons of the olive oil, and the cumin and blend until smooth. Season with salt and pepper.

4 Turn the mixture into a shallow serving dish and chill in the refrigerator for 2–3 hours before serving.

5 To serve, mix the reserved olive oil with the paprika and drizzle over the top of the dish. Sprinkle with the parsley and the reserved chickpeas. Accompany with warm pita bread.

cucumber & yogurt dip

ingredients

SERVES 4

1 small cucumber

10 fl oz/300 ml/1^1/$_4$ cups
    authentic Greek yogurt

1 large garlic clove, crushed

1 tbsp chopped fresh mint
    or dill

salt and pepper

warm pita bread, to serve

method

1 Peel then coarsely grate the cucumber. Put in a sieve and squeeze out as much of the water as possible. Put the cucumber into a bowl.

2 Add the yogurt, garlic, and chopped mint (reserve a little as a garnish, if desired) to the cucumber, season with pepper and mix together thoroughly.

3 Chill in the refrigerator for about 2 hours before serving.

4 To serve, stir the cucumber and yogurt dip and transfer to a serving bowl. Sprinkle with salt and accompany with warmed pita bread.

almond & garlic dip

ingredients

SERVES 6

2 oz/55 g day-old bread,
about 2 slices

9 oz/250 g/scant 1^1/$_2$ cups
almonds

4–6 large garlic cloves,
coarsely chopped

5 fl oz/150 ml/^{2}/$_3$ cup extra-
virgin olive oil

2 tbsp white wine vinegar

salt and pepper

fresh cilantro or flat-leaf
parsley sprigs, to garnish

sesame breadsticks, to serve

method

1 Cut the crusts off the bread and tear the bread into small pieces. Put in a bowl, pour over enough water to cover, and set aside to soak for 10–15 minutes. Squeeze the bread dry, then set aside.

2 To blanch the almonds, put them in a heatproof bowl and pour over just enough boiling water to cover. Let stand for 30 seconds, then drain. The skins should slide off easily.

3 Transfer the almonds and garlic to a food processor and process until finely chopped. Add the squeezed bread and process again until well blended.

4 With the motor running, gradually add the olive oil through the feeder tube in a thin, steady stream until a thick paste forms. Add the vinegar and process again. Season with salt and pepper to taste.

5 Scrape the mixture into a bowl, cover, and chill until required. It will keep in the refrigerator for up to 4 days. To serve, garnish with sprigs of herbs. Serve with sesame breadsticks.

eggplant & garlic dip

ingredients

SERVES 6

2 large eggplants

2 fl oz/50 ml/$1/4$ cup extra-
    virgin olive oil

juice of $1/2$ lemon

5 fl oz/150 ml/$2/3$ cup
    authentic Greek yogurt

2 garlic cloves, crushed

pinch of ground cumin

salt and pepper

chopped fresh flat-leaf
    parsley, to garnish

strips of red and green bell
    pepper or sesame
    crackers, to serve

method

1 Prick the skins of the eggplants with a fork and put on a cookie sheet. Bake in a preheated oven, 375°F/190°C, for 45 minutes, or until very soft. Leave to cool slightly, then cut the eggplants in half lengthwise and scoop out the flesh.

2 Heat the oil in a large, heavy skillet, add the eggplant flesh, and fry for 5 minutes. Put the eggplant mixture into a food processor, add the lemon juice, and blend until smooth. Gradually add the yogurt, then the garlic and cumin. Season with salt and pepper.

3 Pour the mixture into a serving bowl and chill in the refrigerator for at least 1 hour.

4 Garnish with chopped fresh parsley and serve with strips of raw bell pepper or sesame crackers.

split pea dip

ingredients

SERVES 6

9 oz/250 g/generous 1 cup
    yellow split peas

2 small onions, 1 chopped
    coarsely and 1 chopped
    very finely

1 garlic clove, chopped
    coarsely

6 tbsp extra-virgin olive oil

1 tbsp chopped fresh oregano

salt and pepper

warm pita bread, to serve

method

1 Rinse the split peas under cold running water. Put in a pan and add the coarsely chopped onion, the garlic, and plenty of cold water. Bring to a boil then simmer for about 45 minutes, until very tender.

2 Drain the split peas, reserving a little of the cooking liquid, and put in a food processor. Add 5 tablespoons of the olive oil and blend until smooth. If the mixture seems too dry, add enough of the reserved liquid to form a smooth, thick purée. Add the oregano and season with salt and pepper.

3 Pour the mixture into a serving bowl and sprinkle with the finely chopped onion and extra oregano if desired. Drizzle over the remaining olive oil.

4 Serve warm or cold with pita bread.

greek garlic sauce

ingredients

SERVES 6–8

4 oz/115 g/²/₃ cup whole
blanched almonds

3 tbsp fresh white bread
crumbs

2 large garlic cloves, crushed

2 tsp lemon juice

salt and pepper

5 fl oz/150 ml/²/₃ cup extra-
virgin olive oil

4 tbsp hot water

pita bread and raw vegetables
such as bell peppers,
cucumber, and carrots,
to serve

method

1 Put the almonds in a food processor and process until finely ground. Add the bread crumbs, garlic, lemon juice, salt, and pepper and mix together well.

2 With the machine running, very slowly pour in the oil to form a smooth, thick mixture. When all the oil has been added, blend in the water.

3 Pour the mixture into a serving bowl and chill in the refrigerator for at least 2 hours.

4 Serve with pita bread and raw vegetables.

greek sausages

ingredients

MAKES ABOUT 24

12 oz/350 g/1^1/$_2$ cups
   ground pork
4 oz/115 g/ ^{1}/$_2$ cup
   ground beef
1 garlic clove, crushed
^{1}/$_2$ tsp ground cinnamon
^{1}/$_4$ tsp dried savory or thyme
grated rind of 1 small orange
8 black peppercorns, crushed
3^1/$_2$ fl oz/100 ml/^{1}/$_3$ cup dry
   red wine
lemon wedges, to garnish

method

1 Put all the ingredients except the lemon wedges in a bowl and mix well together. Cover and let marinate in the refrigerator overnight or for about 12 hours.

2 Preheat the broiler. Stir the mixture and then, with damp hands, form into about 24 small sausage shapes, about 2 inches/ 5 cm long, and place on a broiler pan.

3 Broil the sausages for about 15 minutes, turning several times, until brown on all sides.

4 Serve hot, garnished with lemon wedges.

deep-fried squid

ingredients

SERVES 6

2 lb/900 g small cleaned
   squid
4 oz/115 g/³/₄ cup all-purpose
   flour
salt and pepper
sunflower oil, for deep-frying

method

1 Rinse and dry the squid. Slice the bodies into rings, leaving the tentacles whole. Season the flour with salt and pepper. Dip the pieces of squid in the flour, making sure they are well coated, then shake off any excess.

2 Heat the oil in a deep-fat fryer to 350°F/180°C, or when a cube of bread, dropped into the fat, turns brown in 1 minute. When the oil is hot, add the squid in small batches and fry for about 1 minute, until crisp and golden. Remove from the fryer with a slotted spoon and drain on paper towels. Continue to cook the remaining squid in small batches.

3 Sprinkle lightly with salt and serve hot.

stuffed vine leaves

ingredients

MAKES ABOUT 30

8-oz/225-g package vine
    leaves preserved in brine
4 oz/115 g/^{2}/$_3$ cup arborio or
    other short-grain rice
6 fl oz/175ml/^{3}/$_4$ cup olive oil
1 small onion, chopped finely
1 garlic clove, chopped finely
2 oz/55 g/^{1}/$_3$ cup pine nuts,
    chopped
2 oz/55 g/^{1}/$_3$ cup currants
3 scallions, chopped finely
1 tbsp chopped fresh mint
1 tbsp chopped fresh dill
2 tbsp chopped fresh flat-leaf
    parsley
salt and pepper
juice of 1 lemon
lemon wedges and authentic
    Greek yogurt, to serve

method

1 Place the vine leaves in a bowl, add boiling water, and soak for 20 minutes. Drain, soak in cold water for 20 minutes, and drain again.

2 Meanwhile, cover the rice with cold water in a pan, bring to the boil, then simmer for 15–20 minutes, or until tender. Drain well and set aside in a bowl to cool.

3 Heat 2 tablespoons of the oil in a skillet and fry the onion and garlic until softened. Add to the rice with the pine nuts, currants, scallions, mint, dill, and parsley. Season with a little salt and plenty of pepper, and mix together well.

4 Place one vine leaf, vein-side upward, on a work surface. Put a little filling on the base of the leaf and fold up the bottom end of the leaf. Fold in the sides, then roll up the leaf around the filling. Squeeze gently to seal. Fill and roll the remaining leaves, then pack the stuffed leaves close together in a large flameproof casserole, seam-side down and in a single layer.

5 Mix the remaining oil and the lemon juice with 5 fl oz/150 ml/^{2}/$_3$ cup water and pour into the casserole. Place a large plate over the vine leaves to keep them in place then cover the casserole with a lid. Bring to simmering point then simmer for 45 minutes. Leave the vine leaves to cool in the liquid.

6 Serve warm or chilled, with lemon wedges and yogurt.

greek beans

ingredients

SERVES 4

14 oz/400 g canned
    cannellini beans, drained
    and rinsed
1 tbsp olive oil
3 garlic cloves, crushed
15 fl oz/425 ml/scant 2 cups
    vegetable stock
1 bay leaf
2 fresh oregano sprigs
1 tbsp tomato paste
juice of 1 lemon
1 small red onion, chopped
1 oz/25 g/generous $\frac{1}{8}$ cup
    pitted black Greek
    olives, halved
salt and pepper

method

1 Put the beans in an ovenproof casserole over low heat, add the oil and garlic, and cook, stirring frequently, for 4–5 minutes.

2 Add the stock, bay leaf, oregano, tomato paste, lemon juice, and onion and stir well to mix. Cover and let simmer for 1 hour, or until the sauce has thickened.

3 Stir in the olives, then season to taste with salt and pepper.

4 This dish is delicious served either warm or cold.

hot roasted nuts

ingredients

MAKES 8 OZ/225 G

2 tbsp olive oil

8 oz/225 g/scant 1¹/₂ cups
   shelled pistachio nuts,
   almonds, or walnut halves

3 tbsp chopped fresh sage,
   thyme, marjoram, or
   oregano

1 tsp paprika or cumin

salt

method

1 Put the oil in a roasting pan and swirl around to cover the bottom. Add the nuts and toss to coat evenly in the oil, then spread out in a single layer. Sprinkle with the herbs, paprika or cumin, and salt.

2 Bake in a preheated oven, 325°F/170°C, for 20 minutes, tossing the nuts occasionally as they cook.

3 Drain, if necessary, on paper towels, and serve warm.

olive bread

ingredients

MAKES 2 MEDIUM LOAVES

2 lb/900 g/8 cups strong
   white bread flour
1 package dry yeast
3 tsp sesame seeds
1 tsp salt
$1/2$ tsp dried oregano
3 tbsp olive oil, plus extra
   for brushing
1 pint/600 ml/$2^1/2$ cups
   warm water
8 oz/225 g/1 cup Greek
   olives, pitted and
   chopped coarsely

method

1 Put the flour, yeast, 2 teaspoons of the sesame seeds, the salt, and oregano in a large bowl and mix. Add 3 tablespoons of the olive oil and, using a wooden spoon, gradually add the water to form a firm dough.

2 Turn the dough onto a lightly floured work surface and knead for 10 minutes, until smooth. Put the dough in a clean bowl, cover with a clean, damp dish towel, and let rise in a warm place for about 1 hour, until doubled in size.

3 Turn onto a lightly floured surface and knead lightly to knock out the air then knead in the olives. Divide the dough into 2 pieces, and shape each piece into a smooth round. Place on a lightly oiled cookie sheet, cover with a clean dish towel, and set in a warm place for about 30 minutes, until doubled in size.

4 Using a sharp knife, make slashes across the top of each loaf then lightly brush with olive oil and sprinkle the remaining sesame seeds on top.

5 Bake in a preheated oven, 425°F/220°C, for 10 minutes then reduce the temperature to 375°F/190°C and bake for another 25 minutes or until risen and brown and the bread sounds hollow when tapped on the bottom. Cool on a wire rack.

walnut cheese wafers

ingredients

MAKES ABOUT 38

1¹/₂ oz/40 g/¹/₄ cup
 walnut pieces
4 oz/115 g/³/₄ cup plus 1 tbsp
 all-purpose flour
salt and pepper
4 oz/115 g butter
4 oz/115 g authentic Greek
 feta cheese
beaten egg, for glazing

method

1 Put the walnuts in a food processor and chop finely. Remove from the processor and set aside.

2 Add the flour, salt, and pepper to the processor bowl. Cut the butter into small pieces, add to the flour, and mix in short bursts, until the mixture resembles fine bread crumbs. Coarsely grate in the cheese, add the reserved walnuts, and mix quickly to form a dough.

3 Turn the mixture onto a lightly floured surface and roll out thinly. Using a 2¹/₄-inch/6-cm round cookie cutter, cut the dough into rounds and place on cookie sheets. Brush the tops with beaten egg.

4 Bake the wafers in a preheated oven, 375°F/190°C, for about 10 minutes, until golden. Cool on a wire rack.

5 Store in an airtight tin.

sesame crackers

ingredients

MAKES ABOUT 30

5^{1}/$_{2}$ oz/150 g/^{2}/$_{3}$ cup plus
   1 tbsp all-purpose flour

3 tbsp sesame seeds

finely grated rind of 1 lemon

2 tbsp chopped fresh thyme

^{1}/$_{2}$ tsp salt

freshly ground pepper

2 tbsp butter

3–4 tbsp cold water

1 small egg white

method

1 Put the flour, 2 tablespoons of the sesame seeds, the lemon rind, thyme, salt, and pepper in a bowl. Cut the butter into small pieces and rub into the mixture until it resembles fine bread crumbs. Gradually stir in the water until the mixture forms a firm dough.

2 Turn the mixture onto a lightly floured surface and roll out thinly. Using a 2-inch/5-cm round cookie cutter, cut the dough into rounds and place on cookie sheets.

3 Brush the crackers with the egg white and sprinkle with the remaining sesame seeds. Bake in in a preheated oven, 375°F/190°C, for 20–25 minutes, until lightly browned. Cool on a wire rack.

4 Store the crackers in an airtight tin.

greek feta & olive tartlets

ingredients

MAKES 12

butter, for greasing

all-purpose flour, for dusting

6 oz/175 g pie dough

1 egg

3 egg yolks

10 fl oz/300 ml/1$\frac{1}{4}$ cups
    whipping cream

salt and pepper

4 oz/115 g authentic Greek
    feta cheese

6 pitted black Greek
    olives, halved

12 small fresh rosemary sprigs

method

1 Grease 12 individual 2$\frac{1}{2}$-inch/6-cm tart pans, or the cups in a 12-hole muffin pan.

2 On a floured counter, roll out the pie dough to $\frac{1}{8}$ inch/3 mm thick. Cut the dough into rounds, use to line the prepared pans, and prick the bottoms with a fork. Press a square of foil into each tartlet shell and bake in the preheated oven for 12 minutes. Remove the foil and bake for an additional 3 minutes.

3 Place the egg, egg yolks, and cream in a bowl, add salt and pepper to taste, and beat together.

4 Crumble the feta cheese into the tartlet shells and spoon over the egg mixture. Place half an olive and a rosemary sprig on top of each tartlet, then bake in a preheated oven, 400°F/200°C, for 15 minutes, or until the filling is just set.

5 Serve warm or cold.

hot cheese pastries

ingredients

MAKES ABOUT 32

7 oz/200 g authentic Greek
 feta cheese

4 oz/115 g/$^1/_2$ cup
 cottage cheese

3 tbsp chopped fresh flat-leaf
 parsley

2 eggs, beaten

pepper

8 sheets authentic Greek filo
 pastry (work with one
 sheet at a time and keep
 the remaining
 sheets covered with a
 damp dish towel)

3$^1/_2$ fl oz/100 ml/scant
 $^1/_2$ cup olive oil

method

1 Crumble the feta cheese into a bowl. Add the cottage cheese, parsley, and eggs, and beat with a fork until well blended. Season with pepper.

2 Cut the filo pastry, down the longest length, into 2^3/4-inch/7-cm strips. Take one strip and brush it with olive oil. Put a heaping teaspoon of the cheese mixture on the bottom left-hand corner. Fold over the corner with the filling so that it meets the long side edge and forms a triangle. Continue folding the filling up and over from side to side to form a neat triangle. Place the pastry on an oiled cookie sheet and brush with oil. Continue until all the pastry strips and the filling have been used.

3 Bake the pastries in a preheated oven, 375°F/190°C, for about 15 minutes until golden brown. Serve hot.

consommé with egg & lemon sauce

ingredients

SERVES 4–6

2$\frac{1}{2}$ pints/1.4 liters/6$\frac{1}{4}$ cups
    chicken stock

2 oz/55 g/$\frac{1}{4}$ cup arborio or
    other short-grain rice

2 eggs

6 tbsp fresh lemon juice

salt and pepper

thin lemon slices, to garnish

finely chopped fresh flat-leaf
    parsley, to garnish

method

1 Pour the stock into a large pan and bring to a boil. Add the rice, return to a boil, then simmer for 15–20 minutes, or according to the instructions on the package, until tender.

2 Meanwhile, put the eggs and lemon juice in a bowl and whisk together until frothy.

3 When the rice is cooked, lower the heat and, whisking all the time, gradually add a ladleful of the stock to the lemon mixture. Pour the mixture into the soup and simmer, still whisking, until the soup thickens slightly. (Do not boil the mixture or it will curdle.) Season to taste with salt and pepper.

4 Ladle the soup into individual serving bowls and garnish with lemon slices and chopped parsley. Serve hot.

fishermen's soup

ingredients

SERVES 6

2 lb/900 g fillets of mixed
   white fish and shellfish,
   such as cod, flounder,
   halibut, monkfish, sea
   bass, whiting, and
   peeled shrimp

5 fl oz/150 ml/²/3 cup olive oil

2 large onions, sliced

2 celery stalks, sliced thinly

2 garlic cloves, chopped

5 fl oz/150 ml/²/3 cup
   white wine

4 canned tomatoes, chopped

pared rind of 1 orange

1 tsp chopped fresh thyme

2 tbsp chopped fresh parsley

2 bay leaves

salt and pepper

lemon wedges, to serve

croutons, to garnish

method

1 Cut the fish into fairly large, thick, serving portions, discarding any skin. Heat the oil in a large pan, add the onion, celery, and garlic, and fry for 5 minutes, until softened.

2 Add the fish and shrimp to the pan, then add the wine, tomatoes, pared orange rind, thyme, parsley, bay leaves, salt, pepper, and enough cold water to cover. Bring to a boil, then simmer, uncovered, for 15 minutes.

3 Serve the soup hot, with lemon wedges, and garnished with croutons.

bean & vegetable soup

ingredients

SERVES 4

8 oz/225 g dried Great
  Northern or cannellini
  beans, covered with water
  and soaked overnight
1 1/2 pints/850 ml/3 3/4 cups
  water
2 onions, chopped coarsely
2 garlic cloves, chopped
2 carrots, chopped coarsely
2 celery stalks, sliced thinly
3 tbsp olive oil
2 tsp chopped fresh thyme
1 bay leaf
pinch of sugar
14 oz/400 g canned tomatoes
  in juice
salt and pepper
2 oz/55 g black Greek olives,
  pitted and chopped
2 tbsp chopped fresh flat-leaf
  parsley

method

1 Drain the soaked beans, rinse under cold water, then put in a large pan. Add the water, bring to a boil, and boil for 10 minutes. Reduce the heat, cover the pan, and simmer for 30 minutes.

2 Add the onions, garlic, carrots, celery, oil, thyme, bay leaf, sugar, and the tomatoes with their juice, breaking them up with a fork. Season with pepper. (Do not add salt at this stage because it will make the beans tough.)

3 Return to simmering point, cover the pan again, and simmer for 45 minutes to 1 hour, until the beans are tender.

4 Season the soup with salt and pepper and serve hot, sprinkled with the chopped olives and the parsley.

roasted vegetable soup

ingredients

SERVES 6

2 eggplants

4 tomatoes

2 red bell peppers

2 onions, unpeeled

2 garlic cloves, unpeeled

4 tbsp olive oil

sprig of fresh oregano

salt and pepper

$2^3/4$ pints/$1^1/2$ liters/7 cups chicken or vegetable stock

fresh basil leaves or chopped fresh parsley, to garnish

method

1 Prick the eggplant skins with a fork and put in a roasting pan. Add the tomatoes, bell peppers, unpeeled onions, and garlic. Sprinkle with 2 tablespoons of the olive oil. Roast in a preheated oven, 350°F/180°C, for 30 minutes, then remove the tomatoes. Roast the remaining vegetables for an additional 30 minutes, until soft and the bell pepper skins have blackened.

2 Put the cooked roasted vegetables in a bowl, cover with a damp dish towel, and leave until cold. When cold, cut the eggplants in half, scoop out the flesh, and put in another bowl. Remove the skin from the tomatoes, cut in half, discard the seeds, and add the flesh to the bowl. Hold the bell peppers over the bowl to collect the juices and peel off the skin. Remove the stem, core, and seeds and add the flesh to the bowl. Peel the onions, cut into quarters, and add to the bowl. Squeeze the garlic cloves out of their skins into the bowl.

3 Heat the remaining olive oil in a large pan, add the vegetables and their juices, the leaves from the oregano, salt, and pepper and cook gently for about 30 minutes, stirring frequently. Add the stock to the pan, bring to a boil, then simmer for 30 minutes.

4 Allow the soup to cool slightly, then purée in a food processor or blender. If necessary, reheat the soup. Serve hot, garnished with basil leaves or chopped parsley.

fresh herb soup

ingredients

SERVES 4

large bunch fresh cilantro

1 pint/600 ml/2¹/₂ cups
    chicken or vegetable stock

1 small onion, chopped
    coarsely

1 large garlic clove, chopped
    finely

finely grated rind and juice of
    1 small lemon

salt and pepper

10 fl oz/300 ml/1¹/₄ cups
    authentic Greek yogurt

method

1 Remove the leaves from the cilantro, reserving the stems, finely chop, and set aside. Coarsely chop the stems. Put the stems, stock, onion, garlic, lemon rind, salt, and pepper in a pan and simmer for 30 minutes.

2 Strain the stock and return to the rinsed pan. Add the lemon juice and yogurt and simmer for 2–3 minutes, until hot. (Do not boil or the soup will curdle.)

3 Add the reserved chopped cilantro and serve hot.

yogurt & tomato soup

ingredients

SERVES 4

4 large tomatoes

2 tbsp olive oil

1 onion, chopped coarsely

1 garlic clove, chopped

10 fl oz/300 ml/1^{1}/$_{4}$ cups
    vegetable stock

2 oil-packed sun-dried
    tomatoes, chopped

1 tsp chopped fresh thyme

^{1}/$_{2}$ tsp ground cinnamon

salt and pepper

10 fl oz/300 ml/1^{1}/$_{4}$ cups
    authentic Greek yogurt

method

1 Coarsely grate the tomatoes into a bowl, discarding their skins left in your hand. Heat the oil in a pan, add the onion and garlic, and fry for 5 minutes until softened. Add the tomatoes and cook gently for an additional 5 minutes.

2 Add the stock, sun-dried tomatoes, thyme, cinnamon, salt, and pepper, bring to a boil, then simmer for 10 minutes.

3 Allow the soup to cool slightly then purée in a food processor or blender, or with a handheld blender. Add the yogurt and mix. Season with salt and pepper.

4 If serving hot, reheat the soup gently. (Do not boil or the soup will curdle.) If serving cold, let cool and then chill in the refrigerator for 3–4 hours.

chilled cucumber soup

ingredients

SERVES 4

2 medium cucumbers

10 fl oz/300 ml/1^1/$_4$ cups
authentic Greek yogurt

10 fl oz/300 ml/1^1/$_4$ cups
chicken stock

2 tbsp walnut oil

1 large garlic clove, crushed

3 tbsp chopped fresh dill

salt and pepper

4 oz/115 g/1 cup walnut
pieces, chopped

method

1 Peel the cucumbers and chop the flesh into small dice. Beat the yogurt with the chicken stock, the walnut oil, garlic, and dill, reserving a little to garnish. Stir in the chopped cucumber and season with salt and pepper.

2 Chill the soup in the refrigerator for at least 4 hours.

3 Stir in the chopped walnuts and serve garnished with the reserved chopped dill.

meat &
poultry

The Greek countryside is not ideal for grazing and for this reason meat is expensive and reserved for festive occasions, of which there are many, as most Greeks observe the saints' days. Making a little go a long way has its advantages, however—some of the most appetizing, best-known, and best-loved classic Greek meat-based dishes, such as the eggplant-layered *moussaka* and the baked pasta dish *pastitsio*, have evolved as a means of making a robust, satisfying dish with only a small amount of meat. Cattle are the most difficult animals to rear successfully, and are often slaughtered young to produce veal. Pigs are more easily reared, but it is sheep and goats that take most readily to the lightly grassed hillsides, and lamb, followed by kid, is the most prevalent and popular meat in Greek cuisine.

Chickens were traditionally kept by all Greek families, and are still to be seen wandering about in mainland villages and on the islands. They are also bred commercially now, and because they are usually free-range and corn-fed, they have an excellent flavor. They are most often served roasted, but chicken kabobs with yogurt sauce is a favorite Greek dish, not to be missed.

moussaka

ingredients

SERVES 4

2 eggplants, thinly sliced

1 lb/450 g/2 cups fresh lean
    ground beef or lamb

2 onions, thinly sliced

1 tsp finely chopped garlic

14 oz/400 g canned tomatoes

2 tbsp chopped fresh parsley

salt and pepper

2 eggs

10 fl oz/300 ml/1¼ cups
    lowfat plain yogurt

1 tbsp freshly grated
    Parmesan cheese

method

1 Dry-fry the eggplant slices, in batches, in a nonstick skillet on both sides until browned. Remove from the skillet.

2 Add the beef or lamb to the skillet and cook for 5 minutes, stirring, until browned. Stir in the onions and garlic and cook for an additional 5 minutes, or until browned. Add the tomatoes, parsley, salt, and pepper, then bring to a boil and let simmer for 20 minutes, or until the meat is tender.

3 Arrange half the eggplant slices in a layer in an ovenproof dish. Add the meat mixture, then the remaining eggplant slices.

4 Beat the eggs in a bowl, then beat in the yogurt and add salt and pepper to taste. Pour the mixture over the eggplants and sprinkle the grated cheese on top.

5 Bake the moussaka in a preheated oven, 350°F/180°C, for 45 minutes, or until golden brown. Serve straight from the dish.

grecian meatballs

ingredients

SERVES 4

1 lb/450 g/2 cups lean, finely
    ground beef or lamb

1 medium onion

1 garlic clove, crushed

1 oz/25 g/$^1/_2$ cup fresh white
    or brown bread crumbs

1 tbsp chopped fresh mint

1 tbsp chopped fresh parsley

salt and pepper

1 egg, beaten

olive oil, for brushing

rice or warm pita bread,
    to serve

method

1 Put the ground beef or lamb in a bowl. Grate in the onion, then add the garlic, bread crumbs, mint, and parsley. Season well with salt and pepper. Mix the ingredients well then add the beaten egg and mix to bind the mixture together.

2 With damp hands, form the mixture into 16 small balls and thread onto 4 flat metal skewers. Lightly oil a broiler pan and brush the meatballs with oil.

3 Preheat the broiler and cook the meatballs under a medium heat for 10 minutes, turning frequently, and brushing with more oil if necessary, until browned. Serve the meatballs with rice or tucked into warm pita bread.

thick beef & pearl onion casserole

ingredients

SERVES 6

2 tbsp olive oil

1 lb/450 g pearl onions,
    peeled and left whole

2 garlic cloves, peeled
    and halved

2 lb/900 g stewing beef,
    cubed

$1/2$ tsp ground cinnamon

1 tsp ground cloves

1 tsp ground cumin

2 tbsp tomato paste

salt and pepper

1 bottle full-bodied red wine

grated rind and juice of
    1 orange

1 bay leaf

chopped fresh flat-leaf
    parsley, to garnish

boiled or mashed potatoes,
    to serve

method

1 Heat the oil in a large flameproof casserole. Add the whole onions and the garlic and fry for 5 minutes until softened and beginning to brown. Add the beef to the casserole and fry for about 5 minutes, stirring frequently, until browned on all sides.

2 Stir the cinnamon, cloves, cumin, tomato paste, salt, and pepper into the casserole. Pour in the wine, stirring in any glazed bits from the bottom, then add the grated orange rind and juice and the bay leaf. Bring to a boil, then cover the casserole.

3 Cook in a preheated oven, 300°F/150°C, for about 1$1/4$ hours. Remove the lid and cook the casserole for another hour, stirring once or twice during this time, until the meat is tender.

4 Garnish with chopped fresh parsley and serve hot, with boiled or mashed potatoes.

braised veal in red wine

ingredients

SERVES 6

4 tbsp all-purpose flour

salt and pepper

2 lb/900 g stewing veal or
   beef, cubed

4 tbsp olive oil

12 oz/350 g pearl onions,
   peeled and left whole

2 garlic cloves, chopped
   finely

12 oz/350 g/2 cups sliced
   carrots

10 fl oz/300 ml/1$\frac{1}{4}$ cups dry
   red wine

5 fl oz/150 ml/$\frac{2}{3}$ cup beef or
   chicken stock

14 oz/400 g canned chopped
   tomatoes with herbs in juice

pared rind of 1 lemon

1 bay leaf

1 tbsp chopped fresh flat-leaf
   parsley

1 tbsp chopped fresh basil

1 tsp chopped fresh thyme

rice, to serve

method

1 Put the flour and pepper in a plastic bag, add the meat, and shake well to coat each piece. Heat the oil in a large flameproof casserole. Add the meat and fry, in batches, for 5–10 minutes, stirring constantly, until browned on all sides. Remove with a slotted spoon and set aside.

2 Add the whole onions, garlic, and carrots to the casserole and fry for 5 minutes, until beginning to soften. Return the meat to the casserole.

3 Pour in the wine, stirring in any glazed bits from the bottom, then add the stock, the tomatoes with their juice, lemon rind, bay leaf, parsley, basil, thyme, salt, and pepper. Bring to a boil, then cover the casserole.

4 Cook in a preheated oven, 350°F/180°C, for about 2 hours, until the meat is tender.

5 Serve hot with rice.

baked pasta with spicy meat sauce

ingredients

SERVES 4–6

2 tbsp olive oil

1 onion, chopped finely

2 garlic cloves, chopped finely

1 lb 7 oz/650 g/2^1/2 cups
    lean ground lamb or beef

14 oz/400 g canned chopped
    tomatoes in juice

pinch of sugar

2 tbsp chopped fresh flat-leaf
    parsley

1 tbsp chopped fresh
    marjoram

1 tsp ground cinnamon

^{1}/2 tsp grated nutmeg

^{1}/4 tsp ground cloves

salt and pepper

8 oz/225 g long, hollow
    Greek macaroni or other
    short pasta

2 eggs, beaten

10 fl oz/300 ml/1^1/4 cups
    authentic Greek yogurt

2 oz/55 g/^{1}/4 cup authentic
    Greek feta cheese, grated

1 oz/25 g/^{1}/4 cup kefalotiri or
    pecorino cheese, grated

method

1 Heat the oil in a pan, add the onion and garlic, and fry for 5 minutes, until softened. Add the lamb or beef to the pan and fry for about 5 minutes, until browned all over, stirring frequently and breaking up the meat.

2 Add the tomatoes, the sugar, parsley, marjoram, cinnamon, nutmeg, cloves, salt, and pepper. Bring to a boil, then simmer, uncovered, for 30 minutes, stirring occasionally.

3 Meanwhile, cook the macaroni in a large pan of boiling salted water for 10–12 minutes or as directed on the package, until tender, then drain well.

4 Beat together the eggs, yogurt, and feta cheese. Season with salt and pepper.

5 When the meat is cooked, transfer it to a large ovenproof dish. Add the macaroni in a layer to cover the meat then pour over the sauce. Sprinkle over the kefalotiri or pecorino cheese.

6 Bake in a preheated oven, 375°F/190°C, for 30–45 minutes, until golden brown. Serve hot or warm, cut into portions.

eggplant cake

ingredients

SERVES 6

6 tbsp olive oil

1 large onion, sliced

2 celery stalks, sliced thinly

1 lb/450 g/2 cups
    ground lamb

3 tbsp tomato paste

5¹/₂ oz/150 g bottled sun-dried
    tomatoes, drained and
    chopped

1 tsp dried oregano

1 tbsp red wine vinegar

5 fl oz/150 ml/generous
    ¹/₂ cup chicken stock

salt and pepper

1 eggplant, sliced thinly

6 tbsp butter

1¹/₂ oz/40 g/scant ¹/₃ cup all-
    purpose flour

1 pint/600 ml/2¹/₂ cups milk

7oz/200 g/generous 1 cup
    kefalotiri or pecorino
    cheese, grated

8 oz/225 g/2 cups dried fusilli

1 tbsp butter for greasing

method

1 Heat 2 tablespoons of the olive oil in a pan over a low heat. Add the onion and celery and cook for 3–4 minutes. Add the lamb and cook, stirring frequently, until browned. Stir in the tomato paste, sun-dried tomatoes, oregano, red wine vinegar, and chicken stock and season to taste. Bring to a boil and cook for 20 minutes.

2 Heat the remaining oil in a skillet over a medium heat. Add the eggplant slices in batches and cook for 4 minutes on each side. Remove and drain.

3 Put the butter, flour, and milk in a pan and heat gently, whisking vigorously with a balloon whisk, until the sauce thickens, boils, and is smooth. Simmer for 1–2 minutes. Remove from the heat. Stir in 5 oz/140 g/generous ³/4 cup of the kefalotiri or pecorino cheese.

4 Bring a large pan of lightly salted water to a boil over a medium heat. Add the pasta and cook until almost done. Drain thoroughly, then stir in half of the cheese sauce.

5 Layer the pasta, lamb sauce, and eggplant slices in a greased dish. Spread the remaining cheese sauce over the top, then sprinkle with the remaining cheese. Cook in a preheated oven at 375°F/190°C, for 25 minutes. Serve hot or warm.

roast lamb with orzo

ingredients

SERVES 4

1 lb 10 oz/750 g boned leg or
   shoulder of lamb

1/2 lemon, sliced thinly

1 tbsp chopped fresh oregano

4 large garlic cloves, 2 chopped
   finely and 2 sliced thinly

salt and pepper

1 lb 12 oz/800 g canned
   chopped tomatoes in juice

pinch of sugar

1 bay leaf

2 tbsp olive oil

8 oz/250 g/1 1/3 cups orzo or
   short grain rice

method

1 If necessary, untie the leg of lamb and open out. Place the lemon slices down the middle, sprinkle over half the oregano, the chopped garlic, salt, and pepper. Roll up the meat and tie with string. Using the tip of a sharp knife, make slits in the lamb, and insert the garlic slices.

2 Calculate the cooking time, allowing 25 minutes per pound plus 25 minutes.

3 Put the tomatoes and their juice, 5 fl oz/ 150 ml/2/3 cup cold water, the remaining oregano, sugar, and bay leaf in a large roasting pan. Place the lamb on top, drizzle over the olive oil, and season with salt and pepper.

4 Roast the lamb in a preheated oven, 350°F/180°C, for the calculated cooking time. Fifteen minutes before the lamb is cooked, stir 5 fl oz/150 ml/2/3 cup boiling water and the orzo into the tomatoes. Add a little extra water if the sauce seems too thick. Return to the oven for another 15 minutes, until the lamb and orzo are tender and the tomatoes reduced to a thick sauce.

5 To serve, carve the lamb into slices and serve hot with the orzo and tomato sauce.

lamb & eggplant moussaka

ingredients

SERVES 6–8

2 tbsp olive oil, plus extra for
  shallow-frying
1 large onion, chopped
  coarsely
1 large garlic clove, chopped
  finely
2 lb 4 oz/1 kg lean
  ground lamb
3 1/2 fl oz/100 ml/1/3 cup dry
  red wine
2 tbsp tomato paste
sugar
1/4 tsp ground cinnamon
1 tbsp chopped fresh oregano
  or 1 tsp dried oregano
1 bay leaf
salt and pepper
3 large eggplants, thinly
  sliced
6 tbsp butter
3 oz/85 g/scant 1/3 cup all-
  purpose flour
1 pint/600 ml/2 1/2 cups milk
1 egg, beaten
1 oz/25 g/1/4 cup kefalotiri or
  pecorino cheese, grated

method

1 Heat 2 tablespoons of the olive oil in a large pan. Fry the onion and garlic until softened. Add the lamb and fry until browned, stirring frequently and breaking up the meat. Add the wine, tomato paste, sugar, cinnamon, oregano, bay leaf, salt, and pepper. Bring to a boil, then simmer, uncovered, for 20 minutes, stirring occasionally.

2 Pour enough oil into a large skillet to cover the bottom, heat, and fry a layer of eggplant slices on both sides until lightly browned.Continue frying the eggplant in batches, adding more oil as necessary. Drain on paper towels.

3 To make the topping, put the butter, flour, and milk in a pan and heat gently, whisking vigorously with a balloon whisk, until the sauce thickens, boils, and is smooth. Simmer for 1–2 minutes. Remove from the heat and allow to cool slightly, then season with salt and pepper and whisk in the egg.

4 Arrange a layer of eggplant in the bottom of a large, ovenproof dish, then spoon over a layer of meat. Repeat until all the eggplant and meat have been used. Pour over the sauce, then sprinkle the grated cheese over the top.

5 Bake the moussaka in a preheated oven, 350°F/180°C, for 50–60 minutes, until golden brown. Serve hot or warm.

lamb & potato moussaka

ingredients

SERVES 4

1 tbsp olive or vegetable oil

1 onion, chopped finely

1 garlic clove, crushed

12 oz/350 g/2 cups lean
    ground lamb

9 oz/250 g/3^2/3 cups sliced
    mushrooms

15 oz/425 g canned chopped
    tomatoes with herbs

5 fl oz/150 ml/^{2}/3 cup lamb or
    vegetable stock

2 tbsp cornstarch

2 tbsp water

1 large eggplant, sliced

1 lb 2 oz/500 g potatoes,
    parboiled for 10 minutes
    and sliced

2 eggs

4^1/2 oz/115 g/^{1}/2 cup soft
    cheese

5 fl oz/150 ml/^{2}/3 cup plain
    yogurt

salt and pepper

2oz/55 g/^{1}/2 cup kefalotiri or
    pecorino cheese, grated

fresh flat-leaf parsley,
    to garnish

salad greens, to serve

method

1 Heat the oil in a pan and cook the onion and garlic for 3–4 minutes. Add the lamb and mushrooms and cook for 5 minutes, until browned. Stir in the tomatoes and stock, bring to a boil, and let simmer for 10 minutes. Mix the cornstarch with the water to a smooth paste and stir into the pan. Cook, stirring constantly, until thickened.

2 Spoon half the mixture into an ovenproof dish. Cover with the eggplant slices, then the remaining lamb mixture. Arrange the sliced potatoes on top.

3 Beat together the eggs, soft cheese and yogurt and season to taste with salt and pepper. Pour over the potatoes to cover them completely. Sprinkle with the grated cheese.

4 Bake in a preheated oven, 375°F/190°C for 45 minutes, until the topping is set and golden brown. Garnish with flat-leaf parsley and serve with salad greens.

lamb with tomatoes, artichokes & olives

ingredients

SERVES 4

4 tbsp authentic Greek yogurt

grated rind of 1 lemon

2 garlic cloves, crushed

3 tbsp olive oil

1 tsp ground cumin

salt and pepper

1 lb 10 oz/700 g lean
     boneless lamb, cubed

1 onion, sliced thinly

5 fl oz/150 ml/^{2}/$_3$ cup dry
     white wine

1 lb/450 g tomatoes,
     chopped coarsely

1 tbsp tomato paste

pinch of sugar

2 tbsp chopped fresh oregano
     or 1 tsp dried

2 bay leaves

3 oz/85g/^{1}/$_2$ cup kalamata
     olives

14 oz/400 g canned artichoke
     hearts, drained and halved

method

1 Put the yogurt, lemon rind, garlic, 1 table-spoon of the olive oil, cumin, salt, and pepper in a large bowl and mix together. Add the lamb and toss together until coated in the mixture. Cover and let marinate for at least 1 hour.

2 Heat 1 tablespoon of the olive oil in a large flameproof casserole. Add the lamb in batches and fry for about 5 minutes, stirring frequently, until browned on all sides. Using a slotted spoon, remove the meat from the casserole and set aside. Add the remaining tablespoon of oil to the casserole with the onion and fry for 5 minutes, until softened.

3 Pour the wine into the casserole, stirring in any glazed bits from the bottom, and bring to a boil. Reduce the heat and return the meat to the casserole, then stir in the tomatoes, tomato paste, sugar, oregano, and bay leaves.

4 Cover the casserole with a lid and simmer for about 1^1/$_2$ hours, until the lamb is tender. Stir in the olives and artichokes and simmer for another 10 minutes. Serve hot.

cinnamon lamb casserole

ingredients

SERVES 6

2 tbsp all-purpose flour

pepper

2 lb 4 oz/1 kg lean boned
    lamb, cubed

2 tbsp olive oil

2 large onions, sliced

1 garlic clove, chopped finely

10 fl oz/300 ml/1¼ cups full-
    bodied red wine

2 tbsp red wine vinegar

14 oz/400 g canned chopped
    tomatoes in juice

2 oz/55 g/⅓ cup seedless
    raisins

1 tbsp ground cinnamon

pinch of sugar

1 bay leaf

salt

paprika, to garnish

topping

5 fl oz/150 ml/⅔ cup
    authentic Greek yogurt

2 garlic cloves, crushed

salt and pepper

method

1 Put the flour and pepper in a plastic bag, add the lamb cubes, and shake well to coat each piece.

2 Heat the oil in a large, flameproof casserole. Add the onions and garlic and fry until softened. Add the lamb to the casserole and fry for about 5 minutes, stirring frequently, until browned on all sides.

3 Pour in the wine, vinegar, and tomatoes, stirring in any glazed bits from the bottom of the casserole, and bring to a boil. Reduce the heat and add the raisins, cinnamon, sugar, and bay leaf. Season with salt and pepper.

4 Cover the casserole with a lid and simmer gently for 2 hours, until the lamb is tender.

5 Meanwhile, make the topping. Put the yogurt into a small serving bowl, stir in the garlic, and season with salt and pepper. Chill in the refrigerator until ready to serve.

6 Serve the casserole hot, topped with a spoonful of the garlic yogurt, and dust with paprika.

lamb with eggplant & black olive sauce

ingredients

SERVES 4

4–8 lamb chops

salt and pepper

3 tbsp olive oil

1 eggplant, cut into $3/4$-inch/
   2-cm cubes

1 onion, chopped coarsely

1 garlic clove, chopped finely

14 oz/400 g canned chopped
   tomatoes in juice

pinch of sugar

16 black Greek olives,
   preferably kalamata, pitted
   and chopped coarsely

1 tsp chopped fresh herbs
   such as basil, flat-leaf
   parsley, or oregano

method

1 Preheat the broiler. Season the lamb chops with pepper.

2 Place the lamb chops on the broiler pan and cook under medium heat for 10–15 minutes until tender, turning once during the cooking time.

3 Meanwhile, heat the olive oil in a pan, add the eggplant, onion, and garlic, and fry for 10 minutes, until softened and starting to brown. Add the tomatoes and their juice, the sugar, olives, chopped herbs, salt, and pepper and simmer for 5–10 minutes.

4 To serve, spoon the sauce onto four warmed serving plates and top with the lamb chops.

lamb with zucchini & tomatoes

ingredients

SERVES 4

4–8 lamb chops

salt and pepper

2 tbsp olive oil

1 onion, chopped finely

1 garlic clove, chopped finely

4 tbsp ouzo (optional)

14 oz/400 g canned tomatoes
    in juice

pinch of sugar

9 oz/250 g zucchini, sliced

2 tbsp chopped fresh thyme

method

1 Season the lamb chops with pepper. Heat the oil in a large, flameproof casserole, add the onion and garlic, and fry for 5 minutes, until softened. Add the lamb chops and fry until browned on both sides.

2 Stir in the ouzo, if using, then add the tomatoes with their juice, the sugar, zucchini, thyme, and salt.

3 Bring to a boil and then simmer for 30–45 minutes, stirring occasionally and turning the chops once during cooking, until the lamb and zucchini are tender. If necessary, add a little water during cooking if the sauce becomes too thick.

4 Serve hot.

rosemary lamb in filo pastry

ingredients

SERVES 4

3 tbsp olive oil

1 small onion, chopped finely

1 garlic clove, chopped finely

6 oz/175g fresh spinach
      leaves

pinch of freshly grated
      nutmeg

2 tbsp authentic Greek yogurt

salt and pepper

4 lamb fillets, each weighing
      about 4 oz/115 g

1 tsp finely chopped fresh
      rosemary leaves

2^1/$_2$ oz/60 g butter

8 sheets authentic Greek filo
      pastry (work with one
      sheet at a time and keep
      the remaining
      sheets covered with a
      damp dish towel)

method

1 Heat 2 tablespoons of the olive oil in a heavy-bottomed pan, add the onion and garlic, and fry for about 5 minutes, until softened. Add the spinach leaves and nutmeg and cook for 3 minutes, stirring.

2 Turn the spinach mixture into a food processor or blender, add the yogurt, salt, and pepper, and blend until smooth. Let cool.

3 Meanwhile, heat the remaining tablespoon of oil in a skillet. Add the lamb fillets and rosemary and fry for 3 minutes on each side. Remove from the skillet, drain on paper towels, and let cool.

4 When the lamb fillets are cool, slash each fillet 4 times, almost all the way through. Fill each slash with the spinach mixture, spreading any remaining mixture on top. Season the fillets with salt and pepper.

5 Melt the butter. Take 1 sheet of pastry and brush with a little of the melted butter. Place a second sheet on top, brush with butter, and fold in half. Put a lamb fillet in the center and wrap to form a parcel. Place on a cookie sheet and brush with butter. Repeat to form 4 parcels.

6 Bake the lamb parcels in a preheated oven, 375°F/190°C, for 25 minutes, until golden. Serve hot.

marinated lamb & vegetable kabobs

ingredients

SERVES 4

juice of 2 large lemons

3^1/$_2$ fl oz/100 ml/generous
   ^{1}/$_3$ cup olive oil

1 garlic clove, crushed

1 tbsp chopped fresh oregano
   or mint

salt and pepper

1 lb 9 oz/700 g boned leg or
   fillet of lamb

2 green bell peppers

2 zucchini

12 pearl onions, peeled and
   left whole

8 large bay leaves

lemon wedges, to garnish

rice, to serve

cucumber and yogurt dip,
   to serve (see page 14)

method

1 Put the lemon juice, oil, garlic, oregano or mint, salt, and pepper in a bowl and whisk together. Trim and cut the lamb into 1^1/$_2$-inch/4-cm cubes and add to the marinade.

2 Toss the lamb in the marinade, cover and refrigerate overnight or for at least 8 hours. Stir occasionally to coat the lamb.

3 When ready to serve, core, seed the bell peppers, and cut into 1^1/$_2$-inch/4-cm pieces. Cut the zucchini into 1-inch/2.5-cm pieces. Thread the lamb, bell peppers, zucchini, onions, and bay leaves onto 8 flat, greased metal kabob skewers, alternating and dividing the ingredients as evenly as possible. Place on a greased broiler pan.

4 Preheat the broiler then put the kabobs under the broiler for 10–15 minutes, turning frequently and basting with any remaining marinade, until cooked.

5 Serve hot, garnished with lemon wedges, with rice and a bowl of cucumber and yogurt dip.

smyrna sausages in tomato sauce

ingredients

SERVES 4

1 lb 2 oz/500 g lean, finely
   ground lamb
2 oz/55 g/1 cup fresh bread
   crumbs
1 onion, chopped very finely
1 garlic clove, crushed
3 tbsp finely chopped fresh
   flat-leaf parsley
1 tsp ground cumin
pinch of ground cinnamon
salt and pepper
1 egg, beaten
2 tbsp olive oil

tomato sauce

1 lb 12 oz/800 g canned
   chopped tomatoes in juice
1/4 tsp sugar
2 fl oz/50 ml/1/4 cup olive oil
1 garlic clove, crushed
1/4 tsp ground cumin
1 tbsp chopped fresh
   flat-leaf parsley
1 bay leaf
salt and pepper

method

1 To make the sausages, put the ground lamb, bread crumbs, onion, garlic, parsley, cumin, cinnamon, salt, and pepper in a bowl and mix together.

2 Stir in the beaten egg, then knead the mixture for about 5 minutes, until it forms a paste. Let chill in the refrigerator for about 1 hour.

3 Meanwhile, prepare the tomato sauce. Put all the ingredients in a large pan (it needs to be large enough to hold the sausages in a single layer). Bring to a boil, then simmer for about 30 minutes.

4 With dampened hands, form the lamb mixture into 12 equal-size sausage shapes, each about 3 1/2 inches/9 cm long. Heat the oil in a large skillet, add the sausages, and fry for 15 minutes, until browned on all sides.

5 Using a slotted spoon, transfer the sausages to the pan containing the tomato sauce and simmer for 10–15 minutes. Serve hot.

lamb's liver in red wine & orange sauce

ingredients

SERVES 4

2 oranges

8 thin slices lamb's or
    calf's liver

2 tbsp all-purpose flour

1 tsp paprika

3 tbsp olive oil

6 fl oz/175 ml/³/₄ cup dry
    red wine

2 tbsp chopped fresh flat-leaf
    parsley, plus extra
    to garnish

2 tbsp chopped fresh oregano

salt and pepper

pasta, to serve

method

1 Using a zester, remove the zest from the oranges. Put the zest in a small pan of boiling water, boil for 1 minute, then drain and set aside. Squeeze the juice from the oranges and set aside.

2 Remove and discard any ducts and membrane from the liver slices. Put the flour and paprika in a plastic bag, add the liver, and shake well to coat each piece.

3 Heat the oil in a large skillet. Add the liver and fry over a medium heat for 4–5 minutes, stirring constantly, until lightly browned all over but still moist in the center. Remove from the skillet with a slotted spoon and place on 4 warmed serving plates.

4 Add the wine to the skillet, stirring in any glazed bits from the bottom. Boil briskly for 1 minute. Reduce the heat and stir in the orange juice, parsley, oregano, salt, and pepper. Heat gently until reduced slightly, then spoon over the liver and garnish with the reserved orange zest and parsley. Serve hot, with pasta.

pork & romaine lettuce in egg & lemon sauce

ingredients

SERVES 4

4 pork loin steaks

salt and pepper

2 tbsp olive oil

bunch scallions, white parts
    only, sliced thinly

1 romaine lettuce, sliced
    thinly widthwise

1 tbsp chopped fresh dill

8 fl oz/225 ml/1 cup
    chicken stock

2 eggs

juice of 1 large lemon

method

1 Season the pork steaks with pepper. Heat the oil in a large, heavy-bottomed skillet, add the scallions and fry until softened. Add the pork steaks and fry for 10 minutes, turning the steaks several times, until browned on both sides and tender.

2 When the pork steaks are cooked, add the lettuce, dill, and stock to the skillet. Bring to a boil, cover, and then simmer for 4–5 minutes, until the lettuce has wilted.

3 Meanwhile, put the eggs and lemon juice in a large bowl and whisk together.

4 When the lettuce has wilted, remove the pork steaks and lettuce from the skillet with a slotted spoon, put in a warmed serving dish and keep warm in a low oven. Strain the cooking liquid into a measuring jug.

5 Gradually add 4 tablespoons of the hot cooking liquid to the lemon mixture, whisking all the time. Pour the egg mixture into the skillet and simmer for 2–3 minutes, whisking all the time, until the sauce thickens. (Do not boil or the sauce will curdle.) Season with salt and pepper. Pour the sauce over the pork steaks and lettuce and serve hot.

pork with fennel & juniper

ingredients

SERVES 4

$^1/_2$ fennel bulb

1 tbsp juniper berries

2 tbsp olive oil

finely grated rind and juice of
    1 orange

4 pork chops, about
    $5^1/_2$ oz/150 g each

crisp salad, to serve

fresh bread, to serve

method

1 Finely chop the fennel bulb, discarding the green parts.

2 Grind the juniper berries with a pestle and mortar. Mix the crushed juniper berries with the fennel flesh, olive oil, and orange rind.

3 Using a sharp knife, score a few cuts all over each pork chop. Place the chops in a roasting pan or ovenproof dish. Spoon the fennel and juniper mixture over the top. Pour over the orange juice, cover and let marinate in the refrigerator for 2 hours.

4 Preheat the broiler to medium. Cook the pork chops under the preheated broiler for 10–15 minutes, depending on the thickness of the meat, or until the meat is tender and cooked through, turning occasionally.

5 Transfer the chops to serving plates and serve with a crisp, fresh salad and plenty of fresh bread to mop up the cooking juices.

braised pork with fennel

ingredients

SERVES 4

1 tsp fennel seeds

grated rind of 1 lemon

salt and pepper

4 pork chops

1 tbsp all-purpose flour

2 tbsp olive oil

2 bunches scallions, sliced
thinly

1 garlic clove, chopped finely

2 fennel bulbs, sliced thinly
with fronds snipped
and reserved

9 fl oz/250 ml/1 cup dry
white wine

1 bay leaf

method

1 Crush the fennel seeds and mix with the lemon rind, salt, and pepper. Spread the mixture over both sides of the pork chops and let marinate for about 1 hour.

2 Dust the pork chops with the flour. Heat the oil in a flameproof casserole, add the pork, and fry until browned on both sides. Remove from the casserole. Add the scallions, garlic, and fennel to the casserole and fry for 5–10 minutes until softened and beginning to brown. Return the chops to the casserole.

3 Pour in the wine, stirring in any glazed bits from the bottom of the casserole, and bring to a boil. Reduce the heat and add the bay leaf. Cover the casserole with a lid and simmer for 45 minutes, until the pork chops are tender.

4 Serve sprinkled with the reserved snipped fennel fronds.

rabbit, roast tomato & sage pie

ingredients

SERVES 4

1 lb/450 g cherry tomatoes

3 tbsp olive oil

1/2 tsp sugar

1 lb 8 oz/700 g boned rabbit, cubed

1 tbsp all-purpose flour

1 onion, chopped

1 garlic clove, chopped finely

3 tbsp pine nuts

5 fl oz/150 ml/2/3 cup chicken or vegetable stock

1 tbsp lemon juice

12 fresh sage leaves, snipped finely

salt and pepper

3 tbsp butter

3 1/2 oz/100 g authentic Greek filo pastry (work with one sheet at a time and keep the remaining sheets covered with a damp dish towel)

method

1 Put the tomatoes in a roasting pan and sprinkle with 1 tablespoon of the olive oil and the sugar. Roast in a preheated oven, 400°F/ 200°C, for 30 minutes.

2 Meanwhile, coat the cubes of rabbit in the flour. Heat 1 tablespoon of the oil in a large, heavy-bottomed skillet and fry the onion and garlic until softened. Add the pine nuts and fry for 1 minute. Using a slotted spoon, transfer the mixture to a 2 1/2-pint/1.4-liter pie dish.

3 Add the remaining oil to the skillet and fry the rabbit for 5–10 minutes, until browned on all sides. Add the stock and lemon juice, bring to a boil, then simmer for 2–3 minutes. Transfer the mixture to the pie dish. Gently stir in the roasted tomatoes. Add the sage and season with salt and pepper.

4 Reduce the oven temperature to 375°F/ 190°C. Melt the butter. Brush one sheet of pastry with butter, cut it into 1-inch/2.5-cm strips, and arrange on top of the pie. Repeat with the remaining pastry sheets, arranging the strips on top of the pie in the opposite direction each time. Make sure the filling is covered and tuck in the edges.

5 Bake the pie in the oven for about 30 minutes, until golden brown. Serve hot.

roast chicken with oregano

ingredients

SERVES 4

3^1/$_2$–4 lb/1.6–1.8 kg whole
   chicken
1 lemon
4 tbsp chopped fresh oregano
1 garlic clove, crushed
2 tbsp butter
3 tbsp olive oil
salt and pepper

method

1 To calculate the cooking time, allow
20 minutes per pound, plus 20 minutes.

2 Grate the rind from the lemon and cut the
lemon in half. Put the chicken in a large
roasting pan and squeeze the lemon juice from
one lemon half into the cavity. Add the lemon
rind, 3 tablespoons of the oregano, and the garlic.
Rub the butter, the juice from the remaining
lemon half, and the oil over the chicken.
Sprinkle with the remaining oregano, salt, and
pepper. Put the squeezed lemon halves inside
the chicken cavity.

3 Roast the chicken in a preheated oven,
375°F/190°C, for the calculated cooking
time, basting occasionally, until golden brown
and tender. (To test if the chicken is cooked,
pierce the thickest part of a thigh with a
skewer. If the juices run clear, it is ready.)

4 Allow the chicken to rest in a warm place for
5–10 minutes, then carve into slices or serving
pieces. Stir the remaining juices in the pan and
serve spooned over the chicken.

spicy aromatic chicken

ingredients

SERVES 4

4–8 chicken pieces, skinned

1/2 lemon, cut into wedges

4 tbsp olive oil

1 onion, chopped coarsely

2 large garlic cloves, chopped finely

4 fl oz/125 ml/1/2 cup dry white wine

14 oz/400 g canned chopped tomatoes in juice

pinch of sugar

1/2 tsp ground cinnamon

1/2 tsp ground cloves

1/2 tsp ground allspice

salt and pepper

14 oz/400 g canned artichoke hearts or okra, drained

8 black Greek olives, pitted

method

1 Rub the chicken pieces with the lemon. Heat the oil in a large flameproof casserole or lidded skillet. Add the onion and garlic and fry for 5 minutes, until softened. Add the chicken pieces and fry for 5–10 minutes, until browned on all sides.

2 Pour in the wine and add the tomatoes with their juice, the sugar, cinnamon, cloves, allspice, salt, and pepper and bring to a boil. Cover the casserole and simmer for 45 minutes to 1 hour, until the chicken is tender.

3 Meanwhile, if using artichoke hearts, cut them in half. Add the artichokes or okra and the olives to the casserole 10 minutes before the end of cooking, and continue to simmer until heated through. Serve hot.

chicken with walnut sauce

ingredients

SERVES 4

4–8 skinned chicken pieces

^{1}/$_2$ lemon, cut into wedges

3 tbsp olive oil

5 fl oz/150 ml/^{2}/$_3$ cup dry white wine

10 fl oz/300 ml/1^1/$_4$ cups chicken stock

1 bay leaf

salt and pepper

3^1/$_2$ oz/100 g/^{3}/$_4$ cup walnut pieces

2 garlic cloves

5 fl oz/150 ml/^{2}/$_3$ cup authentic Greek yogurt

chopped fresh flat-leaf parsley, to garnish

method

1 Rub the chicken pieces with the lemon. Heat the oil in a large skillet, add the chicken pieces, and fry quickly until lightly browned on all sides.

2 Pour the wine into the skillet and bring to a boil. Add the stock, bay leaf, salt, and pepper and simmer for about 20 minutes, turning several times, until the chicken is tender.

3 Meanwhile, put the walnuts and garlic in a food processor and blend to form a fairly smooth purée.

4 When the chicken is cooked, transfer to a warmed serving dish and keep warm. Stir the walnut mixture and yogurt into the pan juices and heat gently for about 5 minutes until the sauce is fairly thick. (Do not boil or the sauce will curdle.) Season with salt and pepper.

5 Pour the walnut sauce over the chicken pieces and serve hot, garnished with chopped fresh parsley.

broiled chicken with lemon

ingredients

SERVES 4

4 chicken quarters

grated rind and juice of
    2 lemons

4 tbsp olive oil

2 garlic cloves, crushed

2 sprigs fresh thyme

salt and pepper

method

1 Prick the skin of the chicken quarters all over with a fork. Put the chicken pieces in a dish, add the lemon juice, oil, garlic, thyme, salt, and pepper, and mix well. Cover and let marinate in the refrigerator for at least 2 hours.

2 To cook the chicken, preheat the broiler or barbecue. Put the chicken in a broiler pan or on the barbecue grill and baste with the marinade. Cook for 30–40 minutes, basting and turning occasionally, until the chicken is tender. (To test if the chicken is cooked, pierce the thickest part of the chicken pieces with a skewer. If the juices run clear, it is ready.)

3 Serve hot, with any remaining marinade spooned over, and garnished with the grated lemon rind.

chicken with goat cheese & basil

ingredients

SERVES 4

4 skinned chicken breast fillets

3^1/$_2$ oz/100 g soft goat cheese

small bunch fresh basil

salt and pepper

2 tbsp olive oil

method

1 Using a sharp knife, slit along one long edge of each chicken breast, then carefully open out each breast to make a small pocket. Divide the cheese equally between the pockets, and tuck three or four basil leaves in each. Close the openings and season the breasts with salt and pepper.

2 Heat the oil in a skillet, add the chicken breasts, and fry gently for 15–20 minutes, turning several times, until golden and tender.

3 Serve warm, garnished with a sprig of basil.

filo chicken pie

ingredients

SERVES 6–8

stock

3 lb 5 oz/1.5 kg whole
    chicken
1 small onion, halved
1 carrot, sliced thickly
1 celery stalk, sliced thickly
pared rind of 1 lemon
1 bay leaf
10 peppercorns

3 large onions, chopped finely
5^{1}/$_2$ oz/155 g butter
2 oz/55 g/scant ^{1}/$_2$ cup
    all-purpose flour
5 fl oz/150 ml/^{2}/$_3$ cup milk
salt and pepper
1 oz/25 g/^{1}/$_3$ cup kefalotırı or
    pecorino cheese, grated
3 eggs, beaten
8 oz/225 g authentic Greek
    filo pastry (work with one
    sheet at a time and
    keep the remaining
    sheets covered with a
    damp dish towel)

method

1 Put the chicken in a large pan with the halved onion, carrot, celery, lemon rind, bay leaf, and peppercorns. Add cold water to cover and bring to a boil. Cover and simmer for about 1 hour, or until the chicken is cooked.

2 Remove the chicken and set aside to cool. Bring the stock to a boil and boil until reduced to about 1 pint/600 ml/2^1/$_2$ cups. Strain and reserve the stock. Cut the cooled chicken into bite-size pieces, discarding the skin and bones.

3 Fry the chopped onions until softened in 2 oz/55 g of the butter. Add the flour and cook gently, stirring, for 1–2 minutes. Gradually stir in the reserved stock and the milk. Bring to a boil, stirring constantly, then simmer for 1–2 minutes until thick and smooth. Remove from the heat, add the chicken, and season to taste. Let cool, then stir in the cheese and eggs.

4 Melt the remaining butter and use a little to grease a deep 12 x 8-inch/30 x 20-cm metal baking pan. Cut the pastry sheets in half widthwise. Line the pan with one sheet of pastry and brush it with a little melted butter. Repeat with half of the pastry sheets. Spread the filling over the pastry, then top with the remaining pastry sheets, brushing each with butter and tucking down the edges.

5 Score the top of the pie into 6 or 8 squares. Bake in a preheated oven, 375°F/ 190°C, for about 50 minutes, until golden. Serve warm.

chicken kabobs with yogurt sauce

ingredients

SERVES 4

10 fl oz/300 ml/1¼ cups
    authentic Greek yogurt
2 garlic cloves, crushed
juice of ½ lemon
1 tbsp chopped fresh herbs
    such as oregano, dill,
    tarragon, or parsley
salt and pepper
4 large skinned, boned
    chicken breasts
8 firm stems of fresh
    rosemary, optional
shredded romaine lettuce,
    to serve
rice, to serve
lemon wedges, to garnish

method

1 To make the sauce, put the yogurt, garlic, lemon juice, herbs, salt, and pepper in a large bowl and mix well together.

2 Cut the chicken breasts into chunks measuring about 1½ inches/4 cm square. Add to the yogurt mixture and toss well together until the chicken pieces are coated. Cover and leave to marinate in the refrigerator for about 1 hour. If you are using wooden skewers, soak them in cold water for 30 minutes before use.

3 Preheat the broiler. Thread the pieces of chicken onto 8 flat, greased, metal kabob skewers, wooden skewers, or rosemary stems and place on a greased broiler pan.

4 Cook the kabobs under the broiler for about 15 minutes, turning and basting with the remaining marinade occasionally, until lightly browned and tender.

5 Pour the remaining marinade into a pan and heat gently but do not boil. Serve the kabobs with shredded lettuce on a bed of rice and garnish with lemon wedges. Accompany with the yogurt sauce.

fish & seafood

The sight of weathered fishermen in little boats landing their catch in a pretty harbor is undoubtedly one of the most appealing to a visitor to Greece. With so many miles of Mediterranean coastline at their disposal, it is hardly surprising that the Greeks feature fish and seafood prominently in their cuisine, and on long summer evenings those harborside villages will have a tantalizing scent in the air of the day's catch being cooked.

The range of species is remarkable and includes sea bass, sea bream, monkfish, red mullet, mackerel, and sardines as well as scallops, shrimp, and octopus and squid. They are cooked in a variety of appetizing ways—roasted, broiled, baked, pan-fried, deep-fried, grilled, stuffed, wrapped in vine leaves—and are often served with classic Greek sauces such as garlic or egg and lemon. Other flavors, such as lemon or lime and wild oregano, complement the fish perfectly, and vegetables are often used in the dish—traditional Greek baked fish, for example, is cooked on a bed of onions, carrots, celery, tomatoes, and herbs. Seafood is also used to make a sauce for pasta, or added to a basic pilaf.

Many of the recipes in this section are suitable for adapting to different fish or seafood, so simply choose your favorite.

fish roasted with lime

ingredients

SERVES 4

2 lb 4 oz/1 kg white fish
    fillets, such as sea bass,
    flounder, or cod

salt and pepper

1 lime, halved

3 tbsp extra-virgin
    olive oil

1 large onion,
    finely chopped

3 garlic cloves,
    finely chopped

2–3 pickled jalapeño chilies
    (jalapeños en escabeche),
    chopped

6–8 tbsp chopped fresh cilantro

lemon and lime wedges,
    to serve

method

1 Place the fish fillets in a nonmetallic bowl and season to taste with salt and pepper. Squeeze the juice from the lime halves over the fish.

2 Heat the oil in a skillet. Add the onion and garlic and cook, stirring frequently, until softened. Remove the skillet from the heat.

3 Place a third of the onion mixture and a little of the chilies and cilantro in the bottom of a shallow ovenproof dish or roasting pan. Arrange the fish on top. Top with the remaining onion mixture, chilies, and cilantro.

4 Roast in a preheated oven, 350°F/180°C, for 15–20 minutes, or until the fish has become slightly opaque and firm to the touch.

5 Serve at once, with lemon and lime wedges for squeezing over the fish.

broiled red snapper with garlic

ingredients

SERVES 4

2 tbsp lemon juice

4 tbsp olive oil

salt and pepper

4 red snapper or mullet,
    scaled and gutted

2 tbsp chopped fresh herbs
    such as oregano, marjoram,
    flat-leaf parsley, or thyme

2 garlic cloves, chopped finely

2 tbsp chopped fresh
    flat-leaf parsley

lemon wedges, to garnish

method

1 Preheat the broiler. Put the lemon juice, oil, salt, and pepper in a bowl and whisk together. Brush the mixture inside and on both sides of the fish and sprinkle on the chopped herb of your choice. Place on a greased broiler pan.

2 Broil the fish for about 10 minutes, basting frequently and turning once, until golden brown.

3 Meanwhile, mix together the chopped garlic and chopped parsley. Sprinkle the garlic mixture on top of the cooked fish and serve hot or cold, garnished with lemon wedges.

traditional greek baked fish

ingredients

SERVES 4–6

5 tbsp olive oil

2 onions, sliced finely

2 garlic cloves, chopped finely

2 carrots, sliced thinly

2 celery stalks, sliced thinly

5 fl oz/150 ml/^{2}/$_3$ cup dry
    white wine

14 oz/400 g canned chopped
    tomatoes in juice

pinch of sugar

1 large lemon, sliced thinly

salt and pepper

2 tbsp chopped fresh
    flat-leaf parsley

1 tsp chopped fresh marjoram

2–3 lb/1–1.3 kg fat whole
    fish, such as sea bream,
    bass, tilapia, or red
    snapper, scaled
    and gutted

method

1 Heat 4 tablespoons of the oil in a large pan, add the onions and garlic, and fry until softened. Add the carrots and celery and fry for 5–10 minutes, until slightly softened.

2 Add the wine and bring to the boil. Add the tomatoes and their juice, the sugar, lemon slices, salt, and pepper, and simmer for 20 minutes. Add the parsley and marjoram.

3 Put the fish in a greased, shallow ovenproof dish. Pour the vegetables around the fish, arranging some of the lemon slices on top. Sprinkle with the remaining oil, and season with salt and pepper.

4 Bake the fish, uncovered, in a preheated oven, 350°F/180°C, for 45 minutes to 1 hour, depending on the thickness of the fish, until tender. Serve immediately, straight from the oven.

roasted fish from spetsae island

ingredients

SERVES 4

2 tbsp olive oil

1 onion, chopped finely

2 garlic cloves, chopped finely

3½ fl oz/100 ml/½ cup dry white wine

14 oz/400 g canned chopped tomatoes in juice

pinch of sugar

2 tbsp chopped fresh flat-leaf parsley

salt and pepper

4 fish fillets, each weighing about 6 oz/175 g, such as sea bass, brill, turbot, cod, monkfish, or tilapia

juice of ½ lemon

2 oz/55 g/⅓ cup dry white bread crumbs

chopped fresh flat-leaf parsley, to garnish

method

1 Heat the oil in a skillet, add the onion and garlic and fry for 5 minutes, until golden. Add the wine, the tomatoes and their juice, sugar, parsley, salt, and pepper, and bring to a boil, then boil gently for about 30 minutes, until the sauce has thickened. If necessary, increase the heat to reduce the liquid.

2 Meanwhile, put the fish in a greased ovenproof dish. Sprinkle with the lemon juice and season with salt and pepper.

3 When the tomato sauce has thickened, spread the sauce over the fish fillets. Roast in a preheated oven, 325°F/170°C, uncovered, for 10–15 minutes, depending on the thickness of the fish.

4 Increase the oven temperature to 425°F/ 220°C. Sprinkle the bread crumbs on top of the fish. Return to the oven and roast for an additional 15 minutes, until the fish is tender and the top light golden brown and crisp. Serve hot, garnished with chopped parsley.

red snapper wrapped in vine leaves

ingredients

SERVES 4

8 small fresh vine leaves or
    8-oz/225-g package vine
    leaves preserved in brine
4 red snapper, each weighing
    about 7 oz/200 g, scaled
    and gutted
salt and pepper
1 lemon, sliced thinly and
    halved
small bunch fresh dill
2 tbsp olive oil

method

1 If using fresh vine leaves, tie them in bundles by their stalks and blanch them in boiling salted water for 1 minute. Rinse under cold running water, dry the leaves, and cut out the stalks. If using preserved vine leaves, place them in a large bowl, add boiling water, and leave to soak for 20 minutes. Drain, soak in cold water for 20 minutes, and then drain again.

2 Season the fish cavities with salt and pepper, then insert some halved lemon slices and 2–3 sprigs of fresh dill in each. Brush the fish with the olive oil and season with salt and pepper.

3 Preheat the broiler. Place 1 fish on 2 fresh, overlapping vine leaves or on 5–6 preserved vine leaves. Roll up the vine leaves and, if using fresh leaves, tie with string.

4 Broil the fish for about 10 minutes, until tender. Serve hot.

fish fritters with greek garlic sauce

ingredients

SERVES 4

4 oz/115 g/³/4 cup plus 1 tbsp
    all-purpose flour, plus extra
    for dusting
pinch of salt
1 egg, beaten
1 tbsp olive oil
5 fl oz/150 ml/¹/3 cup warm
    water
1 lb 8 oz/675 g white fish
    fillets, such as well-soaked
    salt cod, monkfish,
    or cod
sunflower oil, for deep-frying
lemon wedges, to garnish
¹/2 recipe Greek garlic sauce
    (see page 22)
radishes, to serve

method

1 To make the batter, put the flour and salt in a large bowl. Make a well in the center and add the egg and oil, then gradually add the water, beating all the time, to form a smooth batter.

2 Discard any skin and bones from the fish fillets and cut the flesh into chunks, measuring about 2 inches/5 cm square. Dust lightly in flour so that the batter will stick to the fish when it is dipped in it.

3 Heat the oil in a deep-fat fryer to 350°F/180°C, or until a cube of bread, dropped into the fat, turns brown in 1 minute. When the oil is hot, dip each piece of fish in the batter to coat, add to the hot fat in small batches, and fry for about 5 minutes, depending on the thickness of the fish, until crisp and golden. Remove with a slotted spoon and drain on paper towels. Continue to cook the remaining fish in small batches.

4 Serve the fish fritters hot, garnished with lemon wedges and accompanied with the Greek garlic sauce and a bowl of radishes.

skate in mustard & caper sauce

ingredients

SERVES 4

2 skate wings

2 tbsp olive oil

1 onion, chopped finely

1 garlic clove, chopped finely

5 fl oz/150 ml/²/₃ cup
authentic Greek yogurt

1 tsp lemon juice

1 tbsp chopped fresh flat-leaf
parsley

1 tbsp capers, chopped
coarsely

1 tbsp whole-grain mustard

salt and pepper

chopped fresh flat-leaf
parsley, to garnish

lemon wedges, to serve

method

1 Cut each skate wing in half and place in a large skillet. Cover with salted water, bring to a boil, then simmer for 10–15 minutes, until tender.

2 Meanwhile, make the mustard and caper sauce. Heat the oil in a pan, add the onion and garlic, and cook for 5 minutes, until softened. Add the yogurt, lemon juice, parsley, and capers and cook for 1–2 minutes, until heated through. (Do not boil or the sauce will curdle.) Stir in the mustard and season with salt and pepper.

3 Drain the skate and put on four warmed serving plates. Pour over the sauce and sprinkle with chopped parsley.

4 Serve hot, with lemon wedges.

roasted monkfish

ingredients

SERVES 4

1 lb 8 oz/675 g monkfish tail,
   skinned and boned

4–5 large garlic cloves, peeled

salt and pepper

3 tbsp olive oil

1 onion, cut into wedges

1 small eggplant, about 10^1/$_2$ oz/
   300 g, cut into chunks

1 red bell pepper, seeded,
   cut into wedges

1 yellow bell pepper, seeded,
   cut into wedges

1 large zucchini, about 8 oz/
   225 g, cut into wedges

1 tbsp shredded fresh basil

method

1 Make small slits in each monkfish fillet. Cut 2 of the garlic cloves into thin slivers and insert into the fish. Place the fish on a sheet of waxed paper, season with salt and pepper to taste, and drizzle over 1 tablespoon of the oil. Bring the top edges together. Form into a pleat and fold over, then fold the ends underneath, completely encasing the fish. Set aside.

2 Put the remaining garlic cloves and all the vegetables into a roasting pan and sprinkle with the remaining oil, turning the vegetables so that they are well coated in the oil.

3 Roast in a preheated oven, 400°F/200°C, for 20 minutes, turning occasionally. Put the fish package on top of the vegetables and cook for an additional 15–20 minutes, or until the vegetables are tender and the fish is cooked.

4 Remove from the oven and open up the package. Cut the monkfish into thick slices. Arrange the vegetables on warmed serving plates and top with the fish slices.

5 Serve at once, sprinkled with the basil.

fish in egg & lemon sauce

ingredients

SERVES 6

6 fish steaks or fillets, each
    weighing about 7 oz/200 g

1 onion, sliced thinly

7 tbsp fresh lemon juice

5 fl oz/150 ml/$\frac{2}{3}$ cup water

salt and pepper

3 eggs

1 tbsp chopped fresh dill

method

1 Put the fish in a large, shallow pan and add the onion slices, lemon juice, water, salt, and pepper. Bring to a boil, cover the pan, and let simmer for 15–20 minutes, or until the fish is tender.

2 Meanwhile, put the eggs in a bowl and whisk together. When the fish is tender, remove the fish and onions from the pan with a slotted spoon, put on a warmed serving dish, and keep warm in a low oven.

3 Strain the liquid into a measuring cup, then very slowly add to the egg yolks, whisking all the time with a balloon whisk. Pour the liquid into a small pan and heat very gently for 2–3 minutes, whisking all the time, until the sauce thickens. (Do not boil or the sauce will curdle.)

4 Stir the dill into the sauce and season with salt and pepper. Spoon the sauce over the fish and serve hot or cold.

monkfish & shrimp kabobs

ingredients

SERVES 4

1 lb 5 oz/600 g monkfish
1 green bell pepper
1 onion
3 tbsp olive oil
3 tbsp lemon juice
2 garlic cloves, crushed
salt and pepper
16 large fresh shrimp, peeled
16 fresh bay leaves

method

1 Cut the monkfish into chunks measuring about 1 inch/2.5 cm. Cut the bell pepper into similar-size chunks, discarding the core and seeds. Cut the onion into 6 wedges, then cut each wedge in half widthwise and separate the layers.

2 To make the marinade, put the oil, lemon juice, garlic, salt, and pepper in a bowl and whisk together. Add the monkfish, shrimp, onion, and bell pepper pieces and toss together until coated in the marinade. Cover and let marinate in the refrigerator for 2–3 hours.

3 Thread the pieces of fish, bell pepper, onion, and bay leaves onto 8 greased, flat metal kabob skewers, alternating and dividing the ingredients as evenly as possible. Place on a greased broiler pan.

4 Preheat the broiler then broil the kabobs for 10–15 minutes, turning frequently and basting with any remaining marinade, until cooked and lightly charred. Serve hot.

pan-fried fish with lemon

ingredients

SERVES 4

4 tuna or swordfish steaks,
   each weighing about
   7 oz/200 g
salt and pepper
3 tbsp olive oil
juice of 1 lemon
lemon wedges, to garnish
Greek garlic sauce, to serve
   (optional, see page 22)

method

1 Put the fish steaks in a shallow dish and season with salt and pepper. Drizzle over 1 tablespoon of the oil and half the lemon juice. Cover the dish and leave to marinate in the refrigerator for at least 1 hour.

2 When you are ready to cook, heat the remaining oil in a skillet or rub a little over a cast-iron griddle, add the fish steaks and fry for 3–8 minutes on each side, depending on their thickness, until tender. Do not over-cook the fish or it will become dry.

3 Drizzle the remaining lemon juice over the fish steaks. Serve hot, garnished with lemon wedges and accompanied with Greek garlic sauce, if desired.

baked mackerel stuffed with raisins & pine nuts

ingredients

SERVES 4

3 tbsp olive oil

1 onion, chopped finely

3^1/$_2$ oz/100 g/^{2}/$_3$ cup fresh
    bread crumbs

2 oz/55g/^{1}/$_3$ cup raisins,
    chopped

3^1/$_2$ oz/100 g/^{2}/$_3$ cup
    pine nuts

grated rind and juice of 1 lemon

1 tbsp chopped fresh dill

2 tbsp chopped fresh flat-leaf
    parsley

salt and pepper

1 egg, beaten

4 mackerel, each weighing
    about 12 oz/350 g, gutted

salad greens, to serve

lemon wedges, to garnish

method

1 To make the stuffing, heat 2 tablespoons of the oil in a large, heavy-bottomed skillet, add the onion and fry for 5 minutes, until softened. Remove from the heat.

2 Put the bread crumbs, raisins, pine nuts, lemon rind, dill, parsley, salt, and pepper in a large bowl. Add the onion and egg and mix well together.

3 Press the stuffing mixture into the cavity of the fish and place in a greased, shallow ovenproof dish large enough to hold them in a single layer. Using a sharp knife, make diagonal slashes along each fish. Drizzle over the lemon juice and the remaining oil.

4 Bake the fish, uncovered, in a preheated oven, 375°F/190°C, for 30–45 minutes, basting twice during cooking, until tender. Serve hot, on a bed of salad greens, garnished with lemon wedges.

fresh sardines baked with lemon & oregano

ingredients

SERVES 4

2 lemons

12 large fresh sardines, gutted

4 tbsp olive oil

4 tbsp chopped fresh oregano

salt and pepper

lemon wedges, to garnish

method

1 Slice 1 of the lemons and grate the rind and squeeze the juice from the second one.

2 Cut the heads off the sardines and place the fish in a shallow, ovenproof dish, large enough to hold them in a single layer. Place the lemon slices between the fish. Drizzle the lemon juice and oil over the fish. Sprinkle with the lemon rind and oregano and season with salt and pepper.

3 Bake in a preheated oven, 375°F/190°C, for 20–30 minutes, until the fish are tender.

4 Serve garnished with lemon wedges.

deep-fried seafood

ingredients

SERVES 4

corn oil, for deep-frying

7 oz/200 g white fish fillets,
    such as English sole,
    skinned and cut
    into strips

7 oz/200 g monkfish fillets,
    cut into bite-size chunks

4 live scallops, shucked and
    cleaned

8 oz/225 g large cooked
    shrimp, shelled and
    deveined but with tails
    left intact

batter

4 oz/115 g/generous $^3/_4$ cup
    all-purpose flour

pinch of salt

1 egg yolk

1 tbsp olive oil

8 fl oz/225 ml/1 cup milk

2 egg whites

to garnish

fresh flat-leaf parsley sprigs

lemon wedges

method

1 First, make the batter. Sift the flour with the salt into a bowl and make a well in the center. Add the egg yolk and olive oil to the well and mix together with a wooden spoon, gradually incorporating the flour. Gradually beat in the milk to make a smooth batter. Cover and let rest for 30 minutes.

2 Heat the corn oil in a deep-fat fryer, large, heavy-bottom pan, or wok to 350–375°F/180–190°C, or until a cube of bread browns in 30 seconds.

3 Meanwhile, whisk the egg whites in a separate clean, greasefree bowl until they form stiff peaks. Gently fold into the batter.

4 Using tongs, dip the seafood, a piece at a time, into the batter to coat. Deep-fry in small batches for 3–4 minutes until crisp and golden (if you deep-fry too many pieces at a time, the oil temperature will drop and the batter will be soggy). Remove with a slotted spoon and drain on paper towels. Transfer to a warmed serving plate and keep warm in a low oven while you cook the remaining pieces.

5 Garnish with parsley sprigs and lemon wedges and serve.

seafood pasta

ingredients

SERVES 4

3 tbsp olive oil

1 onion, chopped

2 garlic cloves, chopped finely

$3^1/2$ fl oz/100 ml/$^1/2$ cup dry
   white wine

14 oz/400 g canned chopped
   tomatoes in juice

pinch of sugar

2 tbsp chopped fresh herbs
   such as flat-leaf parsley,
   oregano, or marjoram

salt and pepper

14 oz/400 g long, hollow
   Greek macaroni or other
   short pasta

14 oz/400 g frozen seafood
   cocktail, thawed and
   drained

method

1 Heat 2 tablespoons of the oil in a large pan, add the onion and garlic, and fry for about 5 minutes, until softened.

2 Pour the wine into the pan and bring to a boil. Add the tomatoes and their juice, the sugar, chopped herbs, salt, and pepper and simmer for 15–20 minutes.

3 Meanwhile, cook the macaroni in a large pan of boiling salted water for 10–12 minutes or as directed on the package, until tender. Drain the pasta and return to the pan. Add the remaining oil and toss together.

4 Add the seafood to the tomato sauce and simmer for 3–4 minutes, until heated through. Serve the seafood on top of the pasta.

pasta with scallops & pine nuts

ingredients

SERVES 4

14 oz/400 g long, hollow
   Greek macaroni or other
   short pasta
4 tbsp olive oil
1 garlic clove, chopped finely
2oz/55g/$^1/_4$ cup pine nuts
8 large scallops, sliced
salt and pepper
2 tbsp chopped fresh basil
   leaves

method

1 Cook the macaroni in a large pan of boiling salted water for 10–12 minutes or as directed on the package, until tender.

2 About 5 minutes before the pasta is ready, heat the oil in a skillet. Add the garlic and fry for 1–2 minutes until softened but not browned. Add the pine nuts and cook until browned. Stir in the scallops and cook until just opaque. Season with salt and pepper.

3 When the pasta is cooked, drain and return to the pan. Add the scallops and the juices in the skillet to the pasta and toss together. Serve sprinkled with the chopped basil leaves.

shrimp pilaf

ingredients

SERVES 4

3 tbsp olive oil

1 onion, chopped finely

1 red bell pepper, cored, deseeded and sliced thinly

1 garlic clove, crushed

8 oz/225 g/1$\frac{1}{3}$ cups long-grain white rice

1$\frac{1}{4}$ pints/700 ml/3 cups fish, chicken, or vegetable stock

1 bay leaf

salt and pepper

14 oz/400 g peeled cooked shrimp, thawed and drained if frozen

to garnish

whole cooked shrimp

lemon wedges

black Greek olives

to serve

grated kefalotiri or pecorino cheese

cubes of authentic Greek feta cheese

method

1 Heat the oil in a large, lidded skillet, add the onion, red bell pepper, and garlic, and fry for 5 minutes, until softened. Add the rice and cook for 2–3 minutes, stirring all the time, until the grains look transparent.

2 Add the stock, bay leaf, salt, and pepper. Bring to a boil, cover the skillet with a tightly fitting lid, and simmer for about 15 minutes, until the rice is tender and the liquid has been absorbed. Do not stir during cooking. When cooked, very gently stir in the shrimp.

3 Remove the lid, cover the skillet with a clean dish towel, replace the lid, and let stand in a warm place for 10 minutes to dry out. Stir with a fork to separate the grains.

4 Serve garnished with whole shrimp, lemon wedges, and black olives. Accompany with kefalotiri or pecorino cheese for sprinkling on top and a bowl of feta cubes.

made with
vegetables

Greek cuisine is ideal for the vegetarian or for those who simply love vegetables. The richly colored vegetables that are now so firmly associated with the health-enhancing Mediterranean diet—eggplants, zucchini, bell peppers, and tomatoes—flourish under the sunny Greek skies, and form the basis for many tasty dishes. The Greeks also have creative ways of serving vegetables as side dishes—for example, carrots or shallots "à la Grecque" ("in Greek style," cooked in a herb-flavored liquid then chilled), fennel roasted with a crispy topping of bread crumbs, or fava beans served as a salad with feta and scallions in a lemon and olive-oil dressing.

Feta, the deliciously creamy, salty, goat cheese of Greece, marries well with vegetable dishes, as does halloumi, a cheese with a curiously springy texture, which is made of sheep's and goat's milk, or sometimes also with cow's milk, and is especially delicious broiled or fried.

If you only try a few recipes from this section, go for the spinach and feta pie, *spanakópita*, which is sold in various guises in all Greek bakeries, the roasted red bell pepper with halloumi recipe, and of course the not-to-be-missed Greek salad—an uncomplicated, fresh-tasting delight that simply says "Greece."

roasted vegetable moussaka

ingredients

SERVES 4–6

1 large eggplant, sliced
   thickly

2 medium zucchini, sliced
   thickly

2 onions, cut into small
   wedges

2 red bell peppers, cored,
   seeded and chopped
   coarsely

2 garlic cloves, chopped
   coarsely

5 tbsp olive oil

1 tbsp chopped fresh thyme

salt and pepper

2 eggs, beaten

10 fl oz/300 ml/1$\frac{1}{4}$ cups
   authentic Greek yogurt

14 oz/400 g canned chopped
   tomatoes in juice

2 oz/55 g/$\frac{1}{3}$ cup authentic
   Greek feta cheese

method

1 Put the eggplant, zucchini, onions, bell peppers, and garlic in a roasting pan. Drizzle over the oil, toss together, and then sprinkle over the thyme and season with salt and pepper. Roast in a preheated oven, 425°F/220°C, for 30–35 minutes, turning the pan halfway through the cooking, until golden brown and tender.

2 Meanwhile, beat together the eggs, yogurt, salt, and pepper. When the vegetables are cooked, reduce the oven temperature to 350°F/180°C.

3 Put half the vegetables in a layer in a large ovenproof dish. Spoon over the canned chopped tomatoes and their juice, then add the remaining vegetables. Pour over the yogurt mixture and crumble over the feta cheese. Bake in the oven for 45 minutes to 1 hour, until golden brown. Serve hot, warm, or cold.

vegetable moussaka

ingredients

SERVES 4

about 4 fl oz/125 ml/^{1}/$_2$ cup
   olive oil
1 onion, chopped
4 celery stalks, chopped
1 garlic clove, finely chopped
14 oz/400 g canned chopped
   tomatoes
10^1/$_2$ oz/300 g canned green
   lentils
2 tbsp chopped fresh parsley
salt and pepper
1 large eggplant, sliced

sauce

2 tbsp butter
1 oz/25 g/scant ^{1}/$_4$ cup
   all-purpose flour
10 fl oz/300 ml/1^1/$_4$ cups milk
salt and pepper
pinch of freshly grated nutmeg
1 egg
2 oz/55 g/^{1}/$_2$ cup kefalotiri or
   pecorino cheese, grated

method

1 Heat 1 tablespoon of the oil in a skillet over medium heat. Add the onion and cook, stirring frequently, for 5 minutes, or until softened. Add the celery, garlic, tomatoes, lentils and their can juices, and parsley. Season to taste with salt and pepper. Reduce the heat, cover, and let simmer gently, stirring occasionally, for 15 minutes, or until the mixture has thickened.

2 Meanwhile, heat a little of the remaining oil in a large, heavy-bottom skillet. Add the eggplant slices, in batches if necessary, and cook until golden on both sides, adding more oil as necessary. Remove with a slotted spoon and drain on paper towels.

3 Layer an ovenproof dish with the lentil and tomato mixture and the eggplant slices, ending with a layer of eggplant.

4 To make the sauce, put the butter, flour, and milk in a pan over medium–low heat and bring to a boil, whisking constantly. Season to taste with salt and pepper and nutmeg. Remove from the heat, let cool slightly, then beat in the egg. Pour the sauce over the eggplant, sprinkle with the cheese, and bake in a preheated oven, 350°F/180°C, for 30–40 minutes until golden on top.

5 Serve immediately.

stuffed cabbage leaves

ingredients

SERVES 4

8 large cabbage leaves
such as láhana, Chinese
cabbage, or romaine lettuce
1 lb 12 oz/800 g canned
tomatoes in juice
2 tbsp olive oil
2 onions, chopped finely
1 large garlic clove, chopped
finely
2 oz/55 g/$\frac{1}{4}$ cup arborio or
other short-grain rice
2 oz/85 g/$\frac{1}{3}$ cup golden
raisins
1 tbsp chopped fresh mint
10 fl oz/300 ml/1$\frac{1}{4}$ cups
vegetable or chicken stock
2 oz/85 g/$\frac{1}{3}$ cup pine nuts
salt and pepper
1 tsp dried oregano

method

1 Plunge the cabbage into a large pan of boiling water, return to the boil, then boil for 3–4 minutes until softened. Drain well, plunge into ice water, then drain well again. If necessary, cut out any hard cores.

2 Chop 3 or 4 of the tomatoes into small pieces. Heat 1 tablespoon of the oil in a pan. Add half the onions and the garlic and fry until softened and browned. Stir in the chopped tomatoes, rice, golden raisins, and mint.

3 Add the stock, bring to a boil, then simmer for 15–20 minutes, until the rice is tender and the stock has been absorbed. Remove from the heat, stir in the pine nuts, and season with salt and pepper.

4 To make the tomato sauce, heat the remaining oil in a pan, add the remaining onion, and fry until softened and browned. Stir in the remaining tomatoes and their juice, the oregano, salt, and pepper, and bring to a boil, then simmer for about 10 minutes. Allow to cool slightly, then purée in a food processor.

5 Divide the stuffing mixture between the cabbage leaves, and roll up and fold the leaves to form 8 neat packets. Place seam-side down, side by side, in a shallow ovenproof dish and pour over the tomato sauce. Cover the dish and bake in a preheated oven, 350°F/180°C, for 1 hour. Serve hot or warm.

stuffed zucchini with walnuts & feta

ingredients

SERVES 4

4 fat, medium zucchini

3 tbsp olive oil

1 onion, chopped finely

1 garlic clove, chopped finely

2 oz/55 g/^{1}/$_3$ cup authentic Greek feta cheese, crumbled

1 oz/25 g/^{1}/$_4$ cup walnut pieces, chopped

2 oz/55 g/1 cup white bread crumbs

1 egg, beaten

1 tsp chopped fresh dill

salt and pepper

method

1 Put the zucchini in a pan of boiling water, return to a boil, and then boil for 3 minutes. Drain, rinse under cold water, and drain again. Let cool.

2 When the zucchini are cool enough to handle, cut a thin strip off the top side of each one with a sharp knife. Using a teaspoon, carefully scoop out the flesh, leaving a shell to hold the stuffing. Chop the zucchini flesh.

3 Heat 2 tablespoons of the oil in a pan. Add the onion and garlic and fry for 5 minutes, until softened. Add the zucchini flesh and fry for 5 minutes, until the onion is golden brown. Remove from the heat and let cool slightly. Stir in the cheese then the walnuts, bread crumbs, egg, dill, salt, and pepper.

4 Use the stuffing to fill the zucchini shells, and place side by side in an ovenproof dish. Drizzle over the remaining oil.

5 Cover the dish with foil and bake in a preheated oven, 375°F/190°C, for 30 minutes. Remove the foil and bake for another 10–15 minutes or until golden brown. Serve hot.

baked stuffed eggplant

ingredients

SERVES 4

4 large, long, thin eggplants

4 tbsp olive oil plus 5 floz/
150 ml/ $^2/_3$ cup olive oil
or sunflower oil

3 large onions, sliced thinly

2 large garlic cloves, chopped
finely

1 green bell pepper, cored,
seeded, and sliced thinly

14 oz/400 g canned tomatoes
in juice, drained

1 tsp dried oregano

$^1/_4$ tsp dried thyme

4 tbsp chopped fresh flat-leaf
parsley, plus extra to garnish

salt and pepper

2 tbsp lemon juice

method

1 Cut the eggplants in half lengthwise.
Scoop out the flesh, leaving a shell to hold the
stuffing, and reserve. Coarsely chop the
scooped-out flesh.

2 Heat the 4 tablespoons of olive oil in a pan.
Add the onions, garlic, and green bell pepper
and cook for 10–15 minutes until softened,
stirring occasionally.

3 Add the eggplant flesh, the tomatoes,
breaking them up with a fork, the oregano,
thyme, parsley, salt, and pepper. Simmer for
20–30 minutes until the mixture has reduced
and thickened slightly.

4 Spoon the stuffing into the eggplant shells
and place them, side by side, in a shallow
ovenproof dish.

5 Pour the remaining oil around the eggplants.
Add the lemon juice and enough boiling water
to come halfway up the sides of the eggplants.
Cover the dish and cook in a preheated oven,
300°F/150°C, for 1 hour, until tender. Let cool
in the liquid, but do not chill.

6 To serve, lift out the eggplants with a slotted
spoon, discarding the liquid, and garnish with
chopped parsley.

roasted red bell peppers with halloumi

ingredients

SERVES 6

6 small red bell peppers

2 tbsp olive oil

3 garlic cloves, sliced thinly

9 oz/250 g halloumi,
   provolone, or feta cheese,
   sliced thinly

12 fresh mint leaves

grated rind and juice of
   1 lemon

1 tbsp chopped fresh thyme

3 tbsp pine nuts

pepper

method

1 Cut the bell peppers in half lengthwise and remove the cores and seeds. Rub the skins of the bell peppers with a little of the oil, then arrange the bell peppers, skin-side down, on a large greased cookie sheet.

2 Scatter half the garlic into the bell peppers; add the cheese, then the mint leaves, lemon rind, remaining garlic, thyme, pine nuts, and pepper. Drizzle over the remaining oil and the lemon juice.

3 Roast the bell peppers in a preheated oven, 400°F/200°C, for 30 minutes, until tender and beginning to char around the edges. Serve warm.

spinach & feta pie

ingredients

SERVES 6

2 tbsp olive oil

1 large onion, chopped finely

2 lb 4 oz/1 kg fresh young
  spinach leaves, washed or
  1 lb 2 oz/500 g frozen
  spinach, thawed

4 tbsp chopped fresh
  flat-leaf parsley

2 tbsp chopped fresh dill

3 eggs, beaten

7 oz/200 g authentic Greek
  feta cheese

salt and pepper

3¹/₂ oz/100 g butter

8 oz/225 g authentic Greek
  filo pastry (work with one
  sheet at a time and keep
  the remaining
  sheets covered with a
  damp dish towel)

method

1 To make the filling, heat the oil in a pan, add the onion, and fry until softened. Add the fresh spinach if using, with only the water clinging to the leaves after washing, or the frozen spinach and cook for 2–5 minutes, until just wilted. Remove from the heat and let cool.

2 When the mixture has cooled, add the parsley, dill, and eggs. Crumble in the cheese, season with salt and pepper, and mix well.

3 Melt the butter and use a little to grease a deep 12 x 8-inch/30 x 20 cm metal baking pan. Cut the pastry sheets in half widthwise. Take 1 sheet of pastry and use it to line the base and sides of the pan. Brush the pastry with a little of the melted butter. Repeat with half of the pastry sheets, brushing each one with butter.

4 Spread the filling over the pastry, then top with the remaining pastry sheets, brushing each with butter and tucking down the edges. Using a sharp knife, score the top layers of the pastry into 6 squares.

5 Bake in a preheated oven, 375°F/190°C, for about 40 minutes, until golden brown. Serve hot or cold.

zucchini pie

ingredients

SERVES 6–8

2 tbsp olive oil

2 bunches scallions,
    sliced thinly

1³/4 oz/50 g/¹/3 cup arborio or
    other short-grain rice

6 fl oz/175 ml/³/4 cup hot
    vegetable or chicken stock

1lb 10 oz/750 g zucchini,
    grated coarsely and left
    to drain in a colander for
    5–10 minutes

4 tbsp chopped fresh
    flat-leaf parsley

2 tbsp chopped fresh mint

3 eggs, beaten

3¹/2 oz/100 g authentic Greek
    feta cheese

salt and pepper

3¹/2 oz/100 g butter

7 oz/200 g authentic Greek
    filo pastry (work with one
    sheet at a time and keep
    the remaining
    sheets covered with a
    damp dish towel)

method

1 Heat the oil in a pan, add the scallions and fry until softened. Add the rice and cook for 1 minute, stirring to coat in the oil.

2 Add the stock to the pan and simmer for about 15 minutes, until the stock has been absorbed and the rice is tender but still firm to the bite. Remove the pan from the heat and stir in the zucchini. Let cool.

3 When the mixture has cooled, add the parsley, mint, and eggs. Crumble in the cheese, season with salt and pepper, and mix well together.

4 Melt the butter and use a little to lightly grease a deep 12 x 8-inch/30 x 20-cm metal baking pan. Cut the pastry sheets in half widthwise. Take 1 sheet of pastry and use it to line the base and sides of the pan. Brush the pastry with a little of the melted butter. Repeat with half of the pastry sheets, brushing each with butter.

5 Spread the zucchini mixture over the pastry, then top with the remaining pastry sheets, brushing each with butter and tucking down the edges. Using a sharp knife, score the top layers of the pastry into 6–8 squares.

6 Bake the pie in a preheated oven, 375°F/ 190°C, for about 35 minutes, until golden brown. Serve hot.

zucchini slices with greek garlic sauce

ingredients

SERVES 4

1 lb/450 g baby zucchini

3 tbsp all-purpose flour

olive oil, for shallow-frying

grated rind and juice
   of $1/2$ lemon

salt and pepper

$1/2$ recipe Greek garlic sauce
   (see page 22)

method

1 Cut the zucchini lengthwise into $1/4$-inch/ $1/4$-cm thick strips. Dust with the flour to coat.

2 Pour enough oil into a large skillet to cover the bottom, heat, then add the zucchini and fry for 5–10 minutes until golden brown, stirring occasionally.

3 When cooked, add the lemon rind and juice and season with salt and pepper. Serve the zucchini hot, with the Greek Garlic Sauce spooned on top.

artichoke hearts with fava beans

ingredients

SERVES 4

4 tbsp olive oil

1 bunch scallions, white parts
   only, sliced thinly

1 lb/450 g frozen fava beans

$3^1/_2$ fl oz/100 ml/$^1/_2$ cup water

juice of 1 lemon

14 oz/400 g canned artichoke
   hearts, drained and halved

2 tbsp chopped fresh dill

salt and pepper

method

1 Heat the oil in a large pan. Add the scallions and fry for 5 minutes, until softened. Add the beans and stir to coat in the oil.

2 Pour in the water and lemon juice; bring to a boil and boil, uncovered, for 5 minutes.

3 Add the artichoke hearts to the pan and gently boil for 5 minutes, until the beans are tender and most of the liquid has evaporated. Add the dill and season to taste.

4 Serve hot.

carrots à la grecque

ingredients

SERVES 4

1 lb 9 oz/700 g young carrots

2 fl oz/50 ml/¼ cup olive oil

15 fl oz/425 ml/1¾ cups dry
   white wine

1 tbsp Greek honey

2 sprigs fresh thyme

6 sprigs fresh parsley

1 bay leaf

2 garlic cloves, chopped finely

1 tbsp coriander seeds,
   crushed lightly

salt and pepper

chopped fresh herbs,
   to garnish

method

1 Cut the carrots in half and then into quarters to form fingers of equal thickness. Put the carrots and all the remaining ingredients except the chopped herbs in a large pan and bring to a boil, then simmer, uncovered, for about 20 minutes until the carrots are tender.

2 Using a slotted spoon, transfer the carrots to a serving dish. Return the cooking liquid to a boil, and boil until reduced by about half.

3 Strain the cooking liquid over the carrots and let cool. When cool, chill in the refrigerator for 3–4 hours or overnight.

4 Serve at room temperature, garnished with chopped fresh herbs.

braised okra with tomatoes

ingredients

SERVES 4–6

1 lb/450 g okra

5 fl oz/150 ml/²/₃ cup white
  wine vinegar

3 tbsp olive oil

1 large onion, chopped
  coarsely

1 large garlic clove,
  chopped finely

14 oz/400 g canned chopped
  tomatoes in juice

pinch of sugar

salt and pepper

chopped fresh flat-leaf
  parsley, to garnish

method

1 Trim off the tops and tails of the okra but do not cut into the flesh. Put in a bowl, pour over the vinegar, and leave in a warm place for 30 minutes. Rinse the okra well under cold running water and drain.

2 Heat the oil in a large skillet, add the onion and garlic, and fry for 5–10 minutes until softened. Add the okra and fry for about 5 minutes, stirring occasionally, until beginning to brown.

3 Add the tomatoes with their juice, the sugar, salt, and pepper, then simmer for 15–20 minutes, until the okra is tender and the sauce reduced slightly. Do not boil or the okra will burst.

4 Serve hot or cold, garnished with chopped fresh parsley.

greek country beans

ingredients

SERVES 4

6 oz/175 g white beans, such
as Great Northern,
cannellini, black-eyed
peas, or butter beans,
covered with water and
soaked overnight
3^1/$_2$ fll oz/100 ml/^{1}/$_3$ cup
olive oil
1 large onion, chopped
coarsely
1 large garlic clove,
chopped finely
2 carrots, chopped finely
2 celery stalks, finely sliced
14 oz/400 g canned chopped
tomatoes in juice
pinch of sugar
1 tsp dried oregano
1 tbsp chopped fresh
flat-leaf parsley
salt and pepper
Greek olives, to serve
lemon wedges, to serve

method

1 Drain the beans, put in a pan, and cover
with cold water. Bring to a boil, then boil for
10 minutes. Drain and set aside.

2 Heat the oil in a pan, add the onion and
garlic, and fry for 5 minutes, until softened.
Add the carrots and celery and fry for another
10 minutes, until browned.

3 Add the beans, tomatoes, sugar, oregano,
and parsley, and enough boiling water to just
cover the beans. (Do not add salt at this stage
because it toughens the beans.) Bring to a
boil, then simmer for 1–1^1/$_2$ hours, until the
beans are really tender and the sauce is thick.
The beans should be coated in sauce, but add a
little extra water during cooking if the sauce
becomes too thick. (The time will vary, depending
on the type of bean and its age.) Season with salt
and pepper.

4 Allow to cool slightly before serving with olives
and lemon wedges.

crispy roasted fennel

ingredients

SERVES 4–6

3 large fennel bulbs

4 tbsp olive oil

finely grated rind and juice of
 1 small lemon

1 garlic clove, chopped finely

2 oz/55 g/1 cup fresh white
 bread crumbs

salt and pepper

method

1 Trim the fennel bulbs, reserving the green feathery fronds, and cut into quarters. Cook the bulbs in a large pan of boiling salted water for 5 minutes until just tender, then drain well.

2 Heat 2 tablespoons of the olive oil in a small roasting pan or skillet with a flameproof handle, add the fennel, and turn to coat in the oil. Drizzle over the lemon juice. Roast the fennel in a preheated oven, 400°F/200°C, for about 35 minutes, until beginning to brown.

3 Meanwhile, heat the remaining oil in a skillet. Add the garlic and fry for 1 minute, until lightly browned. Add the bread crumbs and fry for about 5 minutes, stirring frequently, until crispy. Remove from the heat and stir in the lemon rind, reserved snipped fennel fronds, salt, and pepper.

4 When the fennel is cooked, sprinkle the bread crumb mixture over the top and return to the oven for another 5 minutes. Serve hot.

shallots à la grecque

ingredients

SERVES 4

1 lb/450 g shallots

3 tbsp olive oil

3 tbsp clear honey

2 tbsp garlic wine vinegar

3 tbsp dry white wine

1 tbsp tomato paste

2 celery sticks, sliced

2 tomatoes, seeded
    and chopped

salt and pepper

chopped celery leaves,
    to garnish

method

1 Peel the shallots. Heat the oil in a large pan, add the shallots and cook, stirring, for 3–5 minutes, or until they begin to brown.

2 Add the honey and cook over a high heat for a further 30 seconds, then add the garlic wine vinegar and white wine, stirring well.

3 Stir in the tomato paste, celery, and tomatoes and bring the mixture to the boil. Cook over a high heat for 5–6 minutes. Season to taste and leave to cool slightly.

4 Garnish with chopped celery leaves and serve warm. Alternatively, chill in the refrigerator before serving.

tomato pilaf

ingredients

SERVES 4

3 tbsp olive oil

1 onion, chopped finely

1 garlic clove, chopped finely

8 oz/225 g/generous 1 cup
long-grain white rice

14 oz/400 g canned chopped
tomatoes in juice

pinch of sugar

1 pint/600 ml/2$^{1}/_{2}$ cups
chicken or vegetable stock

1 tsp dried mint

salt and pepper

2 tbsp pine nuts

lemon wedges, to serve

method

1 Heat the oil in a large, heavy-bottomed pan, add the onion and garlic, and fry for 5 minutes, until softened. Add the rice and cook for 2–3 minutes, stirring all the time, until the rice looks transparent.

2 Add the tomatoes with their juice, the sugar, stock, mint, salt, and pepper. Bring to a boil, then cover the pan with a tightly fitting lid and simmer for about 15 minutes, until the rice is tender and the liquid has been absorbed. Do not stir during cooking. When cooked, gently stir in the pine nuts.

3 Remove the lid, cover the pan with a clean dish towel, replace the lid, and leave in a warm place for 10 minutes to dry out. Stir with a fork to separate the grains.

4 Serve with lemon wedges to squeeze over.

traditional greek salad

ingredients

SERVES 4

6 tbsp extra-virgin olive oil

2 tbsp fresh lemon juice

1 garlic clove, crushed

pinch of sugar

salt and pepper

7 oz/200 g authentic Greek
feta cheese

1/2 head of iceberg lettuce or
1 lettuce such as romaine
or escarole, shredded
or sliced

4 tomatoes, quartered

1/2 cucumber, sliced

12 black Greek olives

2 tbsp chopped fresh herbs
such as oregano, flat-leaf
parsley, mint, or basil

method

1 Make the dressing by whisking together the oil, lemon juice, garlic, sugar, salt, and pepper in a small bowl. Set aside.

2 Cut the feta cheese into cubes about 1-inch/ 2.5-cm square. Put the lettuce, tomatoes, and cucumber in a salad bowl. Scatter over the cheese, and toss together.

3 Just before serving, whisk the dressing, pour over the salad leaves, and toss together. Scatter over the olives and chopped herbs and serve.

salad of greens with lemon dressing

ingredients

SERVES 4

7 oz/200 g mixed baby salad
   greens such as mâche,
   spinach, watercress, and
   wild arugula
4 tbsp mixed chopped fresh
   herbs such as flat-leaf
   parsley, mint, cilantro,
   and basil
about 4 tbsp extra-virgin
   olive oil
juice of about $1/2$ lemon
1 garlic clove, crushed
salt and pepper

method

1 Wash the salad greens and discard any thick stems. Dry and put in a salad bowl. Add the chopped herbs.

2 Make the dressing by whisking together the oil, lemon juice, garlic, salt, and pepper in a small bowl. Taste and add more oil or lemon juice if necessary.

3 Just before serving, whisk the dressing; pour over the salad greens, toss, and serve.

fava bean salad

ingredients

SERVES 4

6 tbsp extra-virgin olive oil

grated rind of 1 lemon and
    2 tbsp lemon juice

1 small garlic clove, crushed

pinch of sugar

pepper

3 lb/1.3 kg fresh young fava
    beans or $1^1/_2$ lb/675 g
    frozen baby fava beans

$5^1/_2$ oz/150 g authentic Greek
    feta cheese

1 bunch scallions, sliced thinly

2 tbsp chopped fresh dill
    or mint

2 hard-cooked eggs,
    cut into fourths

lemon wedges, to serve

authentic Greek yogurt, to serve

method

1 Make the dressing by whisking together the oil, lemon rind and juice, garlic, sugar, and pepper in a small bowl. Set aside.

2 Shell the fresh fava beans, if using, and cook in boiling salted water for 5–10 minutes, until tender. If using frozen fava beans, cook in boiling salted water for 4–5 minutes. Drain the cooked beans and put in a salad bowl.

3 Whisk the dressing and pour over the beans while they are still warm. Crumble over the feta cheese, add the scallions, and toss together. Sprinkle with the chopped dill and arrange the egg fourths around the edge.

4 Serve warm with lemon wedges and a bowl of yogurt to spoon on top, if desired.

charred bell pepper salad

ingredients

SERVES 4–6

2 green bell peppers

2 red bell peppers

2 yellow bell peppers

1/2 tsp cumin seeds or 2 tbsp
   chopped fresh marjoram

5 tbsp extra-virgin olive oil

2 tbsp lemon juice

2 garlic cloves, crushed

pinch of sugar

salt and pepper

Greek olives, to garnish

method

1 Preheat the broiler. Broil the bell peppers, turning frequently, until the skins are charred all over. Put the bell peppers in a bowl, cover with a damp dish towel, and leave until cold.

2 When the bell peppers are cold, hold them over a clean bowl to collect the juices and peel off the skin. Remove the stem, core, and seeds and cut the peppers into thin strips. Arrange the bell pepper strips on a flat serving plate.

3 If using cumin seeds, dry-toast them in a dry skillet until they turn brown and begin to pop. Shake the skillet continuously to prevent them from burning, and do not allow them to smoke. Lightly crush the toasted seeds with a pestle and mortar.

4 Add the toasted cumin seeds or marjoram, the olive oil, lemon juice, garlic, sugar, salt, and pepper to the bell pepper juices and whisk together.

5 Pour the dressing over the bell peppers and chill in the refrigerator for 3–4 hours or overnight. Serve at room temperature, garnished with olives.

tomato salad with fried feta

ingredients

SERVES 4

3 tbsp extra-virgin olive oil

juice of $^{1}/_{2}$ lemon

2 tsp chopped fresh oregano

pinch of sugar

pepper

12 plum tomatoes, sliced

1 very small red onion, sliced
very thinly

$^{1}/_{2}$ oz/15 g arugula leaves

20 black Greek olives

7 oz/200 g authentic Greek
feta cheese

1 egg

3 tbsp all-purpose flour

2 tbsp olive oil

method

1 Make the dressing by whisking together the extra-virgin olive oil, lemon juice, oregano, sugar, and pepper in a small bowl. Set aside.

2 Prepare the salad by arranging the tomatoes, onion, arugula, and olives on four individual plates.

3 Cut the feta cheese into cubes about 1-inch/ 2.5-cm square. Beat the egg in a dish and put the flour on a separate plate. Toss the cheese first in the egg, shake off the excess, and then toss in the flour.

4 Heat the olive oil in a large skillet, add the cheese, and fry over a medium heat, turning over the cubes of cheese until they are golden on all sides.

5 Scatter the fried feta over the salad. Whisk together the prepared dressing, spoon over the salad, and serve warm.

orange & fennel salad

ingredients

SERVES 4

4 large, juicy oranges

1 large fennel bulb, very
thinly sliced

1 mild white onion, finely
sliced

2 tbsp extra-virgin olive oil

12 plump black olives, pitted
and thinly sliced

1 fresh red chile, seeded and
very thinly sliced (optional)

finely chopped fresh parsley

crusty bread, to serve

method

1 Finely grate the rind of the oranges into a bowl and set aside. Working over another bowl to catch the juice, use a small serrated knife to remove all the white pith from the oranges. Cut the oranges horizontally into thin slices.

2 Toss the orange slices with the fennel and onion slices in a large bowl. Whisk the oil into the reserved orange juice, then spoon over the oranges. Sprinkle the olive slices over the top, add the chile, if using, then sprinkle with the orange rind and parsley.

3 Serve with crusty bread.

orange & olive salad

ingredients

SERVES 4

4 thick-skinned oranges

1 small red onion, sliced
very thinly

16 large black Greek olives,
pitted

2 tbsp extra-virgin olive oil

1 tbsp lemon juice

pinch of sugar

salt and pepper

lettuce leaves, to serve

chopped fresh herbs such
as flat-leaf parsley, mint,
or dill, to garnish

method

1 Using a sharp knife, remove the peel and pith from the oranges, then cut the flesh into $1/4$-inch/$1/2$-cm-thick slices, discarding the seeds and white membrane. Put the oranges and any juice, onion slices, and olives in a large bowl.

2 To make the dressing, whisk together the oil, lemon juice, sugar, salt, and pepper and drizzle over the salad ingredients. Gently toss together, then chill in the refrigerator for 2–3 hours.

3 Serve in a shallow dish lined with lettuce leaves. Garnish with chopped fresh herbs.

something sweet

The "something sweet" at the end of a Greek meal is usually a bowl of fresh, seasonal fruit, and there is a truly fantastic selection to choose from—grapes, cherries, figs, apricots, peaches, oranges, tangerines, dates, loquats, apples, pears, melons, pomegranates, and strawberries. Another favorite is the delicious, thick, creamy Greek yogurt served with a drizzle of honey and perhaps a sprinkling of crushed pistachio nuts or almonds. This combination is also made into a wonderful ice cream that is not too sweet.

However, the Greeks do love sweet things, and these are eaten during the day with coffee, or perhaps an hour or two after a meal, rather than as a "dessert." Cakes and cookies also feature seasonal produce such as fruits and nuts, and many are topped with a honey and citrus-fruit syrup that creates an irresistibly soft, moist texture. Greek walnut pastries, *baklavás*, a spicy nut filling in a crisp pastry case steeped in honey syrup, are nothing short of legendary.

The Greeks particularly enjoy their sweet treats on festive occasions, so why not do as they do and make a batch of buttery shortbread cookies which, once cooked, are left to wallow in a bath of confectioners' sugar. They just melt in the mouth—divine!

walnut pastries

ingredients

MAKES 12

$3^{1}/_{2}$ oz/100 g/scant $^{1}/_{2}$ cup
butter
12 oz/350 g/$2^{1}/_{2}$ cups walnut
pieces, chopped finely
2 oz/55 g/$^{1}/_{3}$ cup superfine
sugar
1 tsp ground cinnamon
$^{1}/_{2}$ tsp ground cloves
8 oz/225 g authentic Greek
filo pastry (work with one
sheet at a time and keep
the remaining
sheets covered with a
damp dish towel)
8 oz/225 g/$^{3}/_{4}$ cup
Greek honey
2 tsp lemon juice
5 fl oz/150 ml/$^{2}/_{3}$ cup water

method

1 Melt the butter and use a little to lightly grease a deep 10 x 7-inch/25 x 17.5-cm metal baking pan.

2 To make the filling, put the walnuts, sugar, cinnamon, and cloves in a bowl and mix well.

3 Cut the pastry sheets in half widthwise. Take one sheet of pastry and use to line the pan. Brush the sheet with a little of the melted butter. Repeat with half of the pastry sheets, then sprinkle with the walnut filling. Top with the remaining pastry sheets, brushing each with butter and tucking down the edges. Using a sharp knife, cut the top layers of the pastry into 12 diamond or square shapes.

4 Bake in a preheated oven, 425°F/220°C, for 10 minutes, then reduce the oven temperature to 350°F/180°C and bake for another 20 minutes, until golden brown.

5 Just before the pastries have cooked, make the honey syrup. Put the honey, lemon juice, and water in a pan and simmer for about 5 minutes, until combined. Set aside.

6 When the pastries are cooked, remove from the oven and evenly pour over the honey syrup. Let cool. Before serving, cut along the marked lines again to divide into pieces.

walnut custard tarts

ingredients

SERVES 4

1¹/2 oz/40 g/¹/8 cup butter

8 sheets authentic Greek filo
    pastry (work with one
    sheet at a time and keep
    the remaining
    sheets covered with a
    damp dish towel)

1¹/2 oz/40 g/¹/4 cup walnut
    halves

5 oz/150 g/scant ²/3 cup
    authentic Greek yogurt

4 tbsp Greek honey

5 fl oz/150 ml/²/3 cup heavy
    cream

2 tbsp superfine sugar

2 eggs

1 tsp vanilla extract

confectioners' sugar,
    for dusting

authentic Greek yogurt,
    to serve

method

1 Melt the butter. Brush 4 deep 4-inch/
10-cm tartlet pans with a little of the butter.
Cut the sheets of filo pastry in half to make 16
rough squares.

2 Take 1 square of pastry, brush it with a little
of the melted butter, and use it to line 1 of the
pans. Repeat with 3 more pastry squares,
placing each of them at a different angle. Line
the remaining 3 pans and place the tins on a
cookie sheet.

3 To make the filling, finely chop 2 tablespoons
of walnuts. Put the yogurt, honey, cream,
sugar, eggs, and vanilla extract in a bowl and
beat together. Stir in the chopped walnuts
until well mixed.

4 Pour the yogurt filling into the pastry shells.
Coarsely break the remaining walnuts and
scatter over the top. Bake in a preheated oven,
350°F/180°C, for 25–30 minutes until the
filling is firm to the touch.

5 Let the tartlets cool, then carefully remove
from the pans and dust with confectioners'
sugar. Serve with a bowl of yogurt, if desired.

fig, ricotta & honey tart

ingredients

SERVES 6

pie dough

generous $^3/_4$ cup
   all-purpose flour

pinch of salt

2$^1/_2$ oz/75 g cold butter,
   cut into pieces

scant $^1/_3$ cup ground almonds

cold water

filling

6 figs

$^1/_2$ cup superfine sugar

2$^1/_2$ cups water

1 lb 2 oz/500 g ricotta cheese

4 egg yolks

$^1/_2$ tsp vanilla extract

2 tbsp flower honey, plus
   1 tsp for drizzling

method

1 Lightly grease a 9-inch/22-cm loose-bottom fluted tart pan. Sift the flour and salt into a food processor, add the butter, and process until the mixture resembles fine bread crumbs. Tip the mixture into a large bowl, stir in the almonds, and add just enough cold water to bring the dough together.

2 Turn out onto a floured counter and roll out the dough 3 inches/7.5 cm larger than the pan. Carefully lift the dough into the pan and press to fit. Roll the rolling pin over the pan to neaten the edges and trim the excess dough. Fit a piece of parchment paper into the tart shell, fill with dried beans, and let chill for 30 minutes.

3 Remove the tart shell from the refrigerator and bake for 15 minutes in a preheated oven, 375°F/190°C, then remove the beans and paper. Return to the oven for 5 minutes.

4 Put the figs, half the sugar, and the water in a pan and bring to a boil. Poach gently for 10 minutes, drain, and let cool.

5 Drain any liquid from the ricotta. Stir in the egg yolks and vanilla extract, add the remaining sugar and the honey, and mix well. Spoon into the tart shell and bake for 30 minutes.

6 To serve, cut the figs in half lengthwise and arrange on the tart, cut-side up. Drizzle with the extra honey and serve at once.

honey & lemon tart

ingredients

SERVES 8–12

8 oz/225 g/1¹/₂ cups plus 3
   tbsp all-purpose flour
pinch of salt
1¹/₂ tsp superfine sugar
5¹/₂ oz/150 g butter
3-4 tbsp cold water
13 oz/375 g/1¹/₃ cups cottage
   cheese, cream cheese,
   or ricotta
6 tbsp Greek honey
3 eggs, beaten
¹/₂ tsp cinnamon
grated rind and juice
   of 1 lemon
2 lemon slices, 1 divided into
   eighths, to serve

method

1 To make the pie dough, put the flour, salt, sugar, and butter, cut into cubes, in a food processor. Mix in short bursts, until the mixture resembles fine bread crumbs. Sprinkle over the water and mix until the mixture forms a smooth dough. Wrap the dough in waxed paper or foil and allow it to rest in the refrigerator for about 30 minutes.

2 Meanwhile, make the filling. If using cottage cheese, push the cheese through a sieve into a bowl. Add the honey to the cheese and beat until smooth. Add the eggs, cinnamon, and lemon rind and juice, and mix well together.

3 On a lightly floured surface, roll out the pie dough and use to line a 9-inch/23-cm tart pan. Place on a cookie sheet and line with baking parchment. Weigh down with dried beans and bake in a preheated oven, 400°F/200°C, for 15 minutes. Remove the parchment and dried beans and bake for an additional 5 minutes, until the base is firm but not brown.

4 Reduce the oven temperature to 350°F/180°C. Pour the filling into the pastry shell and bake in the oven for about 30 minutes until set. Decorate with the lemon slices and serve cold.

orange cheesecake with caramelized lemon slices

ingredients

SERVES 8

12 oz/350 g/1½ cups cottage cheese or ricotta cheese

4 egg yolks

4 oz/115 g/²/3 cup superfine sugar

finely grated rind of 1 orange

2 fl oz/50 ml/¼ cup fresh orange juice

2 oz/55 g/½ cup ground almonds

authentic Greek yogurt, to serve

caramelized lemons

2 lemons, sliced thinly

4½ oz/125 g/²/3 cup superfine sugar

5 fl oz/150 ml/²/3 cup water

method

1 Grease and line the base of an 8-inch/20-cm cake pan with removable sides with waxed paper.

2 If using cottage cheese, push the cheese through a sieve into a bowl. Gradually beat the egg yolks into the cheese, then add the sugar, orange rind, and orange juice and beat until smooth. Carefully fold in the ground almonds.

3 Turn the mixture into the prepared pan and bake in a preheated oven, 350°F/180°C, for about 35 minutes, until set. When cooked, turn off the oven, open the oven door, and leave ajar. Allow the cheesecake to remain in the oven for 2–3 hours to cool.

4 Meanwhile, make the caramelized lemons. Put the lemon slices, discarding any seeds, the sugar, and water in a small pan and bring to a boil, then simmer for about 45 minutes, shaking the pan occasionally, until most of the liquid has evaporated and the lemons have caramelized. Watch very carefully toward the end of cooking that the lemons do not burn. Drain the lemon slices on a wire rack.

5 When the cheesecake has cooled, carefully remove from the pan and decorate with the caramelized lemons. Serve accompanied with Greek yogurt.

greek rice pudding

ingredients

SERVES 4

4½ oz/125g/⅔ cup short-
grain rice

10 fl oz/300 ml/1¼ cups
water

1 tbsp cornstarch

1 pint/600 ml/2½ cups
whole milk

3 oz/85 g/⅓ cup superfine
sugar

1 tsp vanilla extract or finely
grated rind of 1 large lemon

ground cinnamon,
to decorate

method

1 Put the rice in a pan and add the water. Bring to a boil, then simmer for 12–15 minutes, stirring occasionally, until the water has been absorbed. Meanwhile, in a small bowl, blend the cornstarch with 2 tablespoons of the milk.

2 Add the remaining milk to the rice, return to a boil, then simmer for 20–25 minutes, stirring frequently, until the rice is very soft and most of the liquid has been absorbed. Stir in the sugar, vanilla or lemon rind, and the cornstarch mixture, return to a boil, then simmer for another 5 minutes, stirring.

3 Spoon the rice mixture into individual serving dishes and let cool. Serve cold, sprinkled generously with cinnamon.

doughnuts in honey syrup

ingredients

SERVES 6

10^1/$_2$ oz/300 g/2 cups plus 2
   tbsp all-purpose flour

1 tsp salt

finely grated rind of 1 orange

1 package dry yeast

10 fl oz/300 ml/1^1/$_4$ cups
   warm water

4 fl oz/125ml/^{1}/$_3$ cup Greek
   honey

1 tsp lemon juice

sunflower oil, for deep-frying

ground cinnamon,
   to decorate

method

1 Put the flour, salt, and orange rind in the bowl of an electric mixer fitted with a dough hook and sprinkle in the yeast. Gradually add the water and whisk for 10 minutes to form a thick batter. Alternatively, make the batter in a large bowl using a whisk.

2 Cover the bowl with a clean dish towel and leave in a warm place for 2 hours, until risen with lots of bubbles.

3 Meanwhile, make the honey syrup. Put the honey, lemon juice, and 1 tablespoon water in a pan and simmer until combined. Set aside.

4 When the batter has risen, heat the oil in a deep-fat fryer to 350°F/180°C or until a cube of bread dropped into the fat turns brown in 1 minute. Using 2 teaspoons (one to scoop and one to push), dip the spoons in cold water to prevent the batter from sticking and drop small amounts of the batter into the hot oil. Cook about 5 at a time, for 2–3 minutes, turning with a slotted spoon, until they puff up and are golden brown. Remove from the fryer and drain on paper towels.

5 Serve about 5 hot doughnuts per person, spoon over the warm honey syrup, and sprinkle with cinnamon.

apricot & pistachio cake

ingredients

SERVES 8–10

$3^1/2$ oz/100 g/$^1/2$ cup ready-
    to-eat dried apricots
finely grated rind and juice
    of 1 large orange
6 oz/175 g butter
6 oz/175 g/$^3/4$ cup plus 2 tbsp
    superfine sugar
4 eggs, separated
8 oz/225 g/1$^2/3$ cups fine
    ground semolina
$3^1/2$ oz/100 g/1 scant cup
    ground almonds

syrup

$5^1/2$ oz/150 g/$^3/4$ cup
    Greek honey
$3^1/2$ fl oz/100 ml/$^1/3$ cup
    orange juice
2 tsp lemon juice

topping

10 oz/300 g/1$^1/4$ cups
    authentic Greek yogurt
1$^3/4$ oz/50 g/$^1/3$ cup shelled
    unsalted pistachio
    nuts, chopped

method

1 Put the apricots, orange rind, and juice in a bowl and let soak for 12 hours. Transfer the apricots and juice to a food processor and blend until smooth.

2 Grease and line a round, 9-inch/23-cm cake pan with removable sides with waxed paper.

3 Put the butter and sugar in a large bowl and beat together until light and fluffy. Add the egg yolks, one at a time, beating well after each addition. Add the semolina and ground almonds and mix well together. Fold in the apricot purée.

4 Whisk the egg whites until stiff, then fold into the mixture. Turn the mixture into the prepared pan and bake in a preheated oven, 350°F/180°C, for about 45 minutes, until light golden brown and firm to the touch.

5 Meanwhile, make the syrup. Put the honey, orange juice, and lemon juice in a pan, bring to a boil, then simmer for 2–3 minutes, until combined. Set aside.

6 When the cake is cooked, let stand in the pan for 5 minutes, then transfer to a wire rack, set over a cookie sheet. Prick the top of the cake all over with a fine skewer. If necessary, reheat the syrup. Spoon the hot syrup over the warm cake and leave on the wire rack to cool. Just before serving, spread the yogurt over the cake and sprinkle with the pistachio nuts.

walnut cake

ingredients

SERVES 12

4 oz/115 g/^{3}/$_4$ cup plus 2 tbsp
self-rising flour

^{1}/$_2$ tsp ground cinnamon

^{1}/$_4$ tsp ground cloves

4 oz/115 g butter, softened

4 oz/115 g/^{2}/$_3$ cup superfine
sugar

4 eggs

8 oz/225 g/1^1/$_2$ cups walnut
pieces, chopped finely

pared rind and juice of
1 orange

4 oz/115 g/^{2}/$_3$ cup white
granulated sugar

2 tbsp brandy

method

1 Grease and line the bottom of a deep metal baking pan measuring 10 x 7 inches/ 25 cm x 17.5 cm with waxed paper.

2 Sift together the flour, cinnamon, and cloves. Put the butter and superfine sugar in a large bowl and beat together until light and fluffy. Add the eggs, one at a time, beating well after each addition. Using a metal spoon, fold in the sifted flour, then fold in the walnuts.

3 Turn the mixture into the prepared pan and bake in a preheated oven, 375°F/190°C, for 30 minutes, until risen and firm to the touch.

4 Meanwhile, put the orange juice in a measuring cup and add water to make 5 fl oz/ 150 ml/^{2}/$_3$ cup. Pour into a pan, add the granulated sugar and the pared orange rind, and heat gently until the sugar has dissolved. Bring to a boil and boil for 6 minutes until the mixture begins to thicken. Remove from the heat and stir in the brandy.

5 When the cake is cooked, prick the surface all over with a fine skewer, then strain the hot syrup over the top of the cake. Leave in the pan for at least 4 hours before serving.

yogurt cake

ingredients

SERVES 8

5 fl oz/150 ml/²/₃ cup
   authentic Greek yogurt
4¹/₂ fl oz/140 ml/¹/₂ cup
   plus 1 tbsp sunflower
   or corn oil
9 oz/250 g/1¹/₂ cups
   superfine sugar
9 oz/250 g/1³/₄ cups self-
   rising flour
2 eggs
finely grated rind and juice of
   2 large lemons
2¹/₂ oz/70 g/¹/₃ cup white
   granulated sugar
2 tbsp Greek honey
1 oz/25 g/¹/₄ cup toasted
   slivered almonds,
   to decorate
authentic Greek yogurt,
   to serve

method

1 Grease and line a round, 8-inch/20-cm cake pan with removable sides with waxed paper.

2 Put the yogurt, oil, superfine sugar, flour, eggs, and lemon rind in a large bowl or food processor and whisk together until smooth.

3 Turn the mixture into the prepared cake pan and bake in a preheated oven, 350°F/180°C, for about 1¹/4 hours, until golden brown and a skewer inserted in the center comes out clean.

4 Meanwhile, put the lemon juice and granulated sugar in a pan and heat gently until the sugar has dissolved. Bring to a boil, then simmer for 2–3 minutes. Stir in the honey.

5 When the cake is cooked, carefully remove from the pan and place on a wire cooling rack, set over a cookie sheet. Prick the top of the cake all over with a fine skewer. If necessary, reheat the lemon syrup, then pour the hot syrup over the warm cake and let cool. Scatter the slivered almonds on top to decorate before serving. Serve with Greek yogurt.

semolina & almond cake

ingredients

SERVES 8–12

8 oz/225 g butter, softened

8 oz/225 g/1 cup superfine
　　sugar

6 eggs, separated

4 oz/115 g/$^3/_4$ cup plus 2 tbsp
　　fine ground semolina

6 oz/175 g/1$^1/_2$ cups ground
　　almonds

finely grated rind and juice of
　　3 oranges

4$^1/_2$ oz/125 g/$^2/_3$ cup white
　　granulated sugar

2 fl oz/50 ml/$^1/_4$ cup water

1 cinnamon stick

finely grated rind and juice of
　　2 lemons

method

1 Grease and line a round, 9-inch/22.5-cm cake pan with removable sides with waxed paper.

2 Put the butter and superfine sugar in a large bowl and beat together until light and fluffy. Add the egg yolks, one at a time, beating well after each addition. Add the semolina, ground almonds, orange rind, and juice, and mix well together.

3 Whisk the egg whites until stiff, then fold into the mixture. Turn the mixture into the prepared pan and bake in a preheated oven, 350°F/180°C, for 50 minutes to 1 hour, until golden brown and firm to the touch.

4 Put the granulated sugar, water, and the cinnamon stick in a pan and heat gently until the sugar has dissolved. Bring to a boil and boil for 4 minutes, until the mixture begins to thicken. Remove from the heat and add the lemon rind. Strain in the lemon juice.

5 When the cake is cooked, let stand in the pan for 5 minutes, then carefully remove and place on a wire cooling rack set over a cookie sheet. Prick the top of the cake all over with a fine skewer. Remove the cinnamon stick from the lemon syrup and, if necessary, reheat the syrup. Spoon the hot syrup and lemon rind over the warm cake, and let cool.

orange & walnut cakes

ingredients

MAKES ABOUT 18

14 oz/400 g/3 cups self-rising
    flour
$1/2$ tsp baking soda
$1/2$ tsp ground cinnamon
$1/4$ tsp ground cloves
pinch of grated nutmeg
pinch of salt
10 fl oz/300 ml/$1^1/4$ cups
    olive oil
$2^3/4$ oz/75 g/generous $1/3$ cup
    superfine sugar
finely grated rind and juice of
    1 large orange

topping

1 oz/25 g/$1/4$ cup walnut
    pieces, chopped finely
$1/2$ tsp ground cinnamon

syrup

6 oz/175 g/$1/2$ cup Greek
    honey
4 fl oz/125ml/$1/2$ cup water
juice of 1 small lemon
juice of 1 small orange or
    1 tbsp orange flower water

method

1 Sift together the flour, baking soda, cinnamon, cloves, nutmeg, and salt.

2 Put the oil and sugar in a bowl and beat together. Add the orange rind and juice, then gradually beat in the flour mixture. Turn the mixture onto a lightly floured surface and knead for 2–3 minutes, until smooth.

3 Take small, egg-size pieces of dough and shape into ovals. Place on cookie sheets, allowing room for spreading and, with the back of a fork, press the top of each twice to make a criss-cross design.

4 Bake the cakes in a preheated oven, 350°F/180°C, for about 20 minutes, until lightly browned. Transfer to a wire rack and let cool.

5 Meanwhile, make the topping by mixing together the walnuts and cinnamon. To make the syrup, put the honey and water in a pan, bring to a boil, then simmer for 5 minutes. Remove from the heat and add the lemon juice and orange juice or orange flower water.

6 When the cakes have almost cooled, using a slotted spoon submerge each cake in the hot syrup and leave for about 1 minute. Place on a tray and top each with the walnut mixture. Let cool completely before serving.

butter cookies

ingredients

MAKES ABOUT 36

6 oz/175 g butter

5oz/140 g/³/₄ cup
superfine sugar

1 egg

10 oz/280 g/2 cups self-rising
flour

finely grated rind of 1 lemon

3 tbsp slivered almonds
(optional)

method

1 Put the butter and sugar in a bowl and whisk until light and fluffy. Whisk in the egg, then fold in the flour and lemon rind.

2 Turn out the dough onto a lightly floured surface and knead gently until smooth. Form the mixture into rolls the thickness of a finger, then cut into 4-inch/10-cm lengths. Shape each roll into an S-shape and place on cookie sheets, allowing room for spreading. If desired, stud with a few slivered almonds.

3 Bake the cookies in a preheated oven, 350°F/180°C, for about 15 minutes, until lightly browned. Cool on a wire rack. Store the cookies in an airtight tin.

greek shortbread cookies

ingredients

MAKES 24

8 oz/225 g butter, softened

2oz/55 g/$1/2$ cup
    confectioners' sugar

1 egg yolk

1 tbsp ouzo or brandy

12 oz/350 g/$2^1/2$ cups
    all-purpose flour

4 oz/115 g/1 cup ground
    almonds

confectioners' sugar,
    for dredging

method

1 Put the butter and confectioners' sugar in a large bowl and beat until pale and fluffy. Beat in the egg yolk and ouzo or brandy and then the flour and almonds to form a soft, firm dough. Using your hands, quickly knead the mixture together.

2 Cut the dough into 24 pieces. Roll each piece into a ball and then into a sausage shape measuring about 3 inches/7.5 cm long. Place the sausage over one finger and press down on the ends to form a plump moon shape. Place on cookie sheets, allowing room for them to spread slightly.

3 Bake in a preheated oven, 350°F/180°C, for 15 minutes, until firm to the touch and light golden brown. Meanwhile, sift a layer of confectioners' sugar into a large roasting pan.

4 When baked, allow the cookies to cool slightly then place in the pan in a single layer, as close together as possible. Sift confectioners' sugar generously on top and let cool for 3–4 hours. Store them in an airtight tin with any remaining confectioners' sugar, so that the cookies remain coated.

pistachio ice cream

ingredients

SERVES 4

$^{1}/_{2}$ pint/300 ml/1$^{1}/_{4}$ cups
    heavy cream
5$^{1}/_{2}$ oz/150 g/$^{2}/_{3}$ cup
    authentic Greek yogurt
2 tbsp milk
3 tbsp Greek honey
green food coloring
1$^{3}/_{4}$ oz/50 g/$^{2}/_{3}$ cup shelled
    unsalted pistachio nuts,
    finely chopped

pistachio praline
oil, for brushing
5$^{1}/_{2}$ oz/150 g/$^{3}/_{4}$ cup
    granulated sugar
3 tbsp water
1$^{3}/_{4}$ oz/50 g/$^{2}/_{3}$ cup shelled,
    whole, unsalted
    pistachio nuts

method

1 Set the freezer to its lowest setting. Put the cream, yogurt, milk, and honey in a bowl and mix together. Add a few drops of green food coloring to tint the mixture pale green and stir in well. Pour the mixture into a shallow freezer container and freeze, uncovered, for 1–2 hours, until beginning to set around the edges. Turn the mixture into a bowl and, with a fork, stir until smooth then stir in the pistachio nuts. Return to the freezer container, cover, and freeze for another 2–3 hours, until firm. Alternatively, use an ice-cream maker, following the manufacturer's instructions.

2 To make the pistachio praline, brush a cookie sheet with oil. Put the sugar and water in a pan and heat gently, stirring, until the sugar has dissolved, then let bubble gently, without stirring, for 6–10 minutes, until lightly golden brown.

3 Remove the pan from the heat and stir in the pistachio nuts. Immediately pour the mixture onto the cookie sheet and spread out evenly. Let stand in a cool place for about 1 hour, until cold and hardened, then put it in a plastic bag and crush with a hammer.

4 About 30 minutes before serving, remove the ice cream from the freezer and let stand at room temperature to soften slightly. To serve, scatter the praline over the ice cream.

lemon ice cream

ingredients

SERVES 4–6

ice bowl

2 lemons

water

ice cream

1 lb 2 oz/500 g/4^{1}/$_{4}$ cups
authentic Greek yogurt

5 fl oz/150 ml/^{2}/$_{3}$ cup heavy
cream

4 oz/115 g/^{2}/$_{3}$ cup superfine
sugar

6 tbsp lemon juice

method

1 To make the ice bowl, thinly slice the lemons and discard the pips. Use the lemon slices to line the base and sides of a 1^{1}/$_{2}$-quart/ 1.7-liter freezerproof bowl. Insert a 1-quart/ 1.1-liter freezerproof bowl inside and fill the space between the two bowls with water. Immediately place a plate and heavy weight on top. Transfer to the freezer and freeze for at least 4 hours, until frozen.

2 Set the freezer to its lowest setting. To make the ice cream, put the yogurt, cream, sugar, and lemon juice in a bowl and mix well.

3 Pour the mixture into a shallow freezer container and freeze, uncovered, for 1–2 hours, until beginning to set around the edges. Turn the mixture into a bowl and, with a fork, stir until smooth. Return to the freezer container, cover, and freeze for another 2–3 hours, until firm. Alternatively, use an ice-cream maker, following the manufacturer's instructions.

4 To use the ice bowl, remove the weight and plate and quickly run the bowls under hot water until they loosen, then remove the ice bowl. Quickly transfer the ice bowl to a serving plate and return to the freezer.

5 About 30 minutes before serving the ice cream, remove it from the freezer and leave at room temperature to allow it to soften slightly. Spoon into the ice bowl and serve.

baked stuffed honey figs

ingredients

SERVES 4

5 fl oz/150 ml/^{2}/$_3$ cup fresh
   orange juice
6 tbsp Greek honey
12 ready-to-eat dried figs
1^1/$_2$ oz/40 g/^{1}/$_4$ cup shelled
   pistachio nuts, chopped
   finely
1 oz/25g/^{1}/$_4$ cup ready-to-eat
   dried apricots, chopped
   very finely
1 tsp sesame seeds
authentic Greek yogurt,
   to serve

method

1 Put the orange juice and 5 tablespoons of the honey in a pan and heat gently until the honey has dissolved. Add the figs and simmer for 10 minutes, until softened. Remove from the heat and let the figs cool in the liquid.

2 Meanwhile, prepare the filling. Put the nuts, apricots, sesame seeds, and remaining tablespoon of honey in a bowl and mix well.

3 Using a slotted spoon, remove the figs from the cooking liquid and reserve. Cut a slit at the top of each fig, where the stem joins. Using your fingers, plump up the figs and stuff each fig with about 1 teaspoon of the filling mixture. Close the top of each fig and place in an ovenproof dish. Pour over the reserved cooking liquid.

4 Bake the figs in a preheated oven, 325°F/ 180°C, for 10 minutes, until hot. Serve warm or cold, with the sauce and Greek yogurt.

almond paste pears

ingredients

MAKES ABOUT 20

oil, for greasing

7 oz/200 g/1³/₄ cups ground almonds

3¹/₂ oz/100 g/¹/₂ cup superfine sugar

2 tbsp fine ground semolina

1 egg, beaten

1 tsp orange flower water or rosewater, plus extra for brushing

about 20 whole cloves

confectioners' sugar, for dusting

method

1 Oil a cookie sheet. Put the ground almonds, superfine sugar, and semolina in a bowl and mix together. Stir in the egg and orange-flower water or rosewater and knead to a smooth dough.

2 Break off small pieces of the mixture, about the size of a walnut, and form into pear shapes. Insert a clove in the top of each to form a stem. Place on the cookie sheet.

3 Bake the almond pears in a preheated oven, 300°F/150°C, for about 20 minutes, until lightly colored. Let cool.

4 When the almond pears are cold, brush lightly with orange flower water or rosewater and then dust with sifted confectioners' sugar.

oranges in caramel sauce

ingredients

SERVES 6

9 oranges
6 fl oz/175ml³/₄ cup water
9 oz/250 g/1¹/₃ cups white
    granulated sugar
3 tbsp Greek honey

method

1 Using a zester, remove the zest from the oranges and put in a small pan. Add the water and leave to soak for 1 hour.

2 When the orange zest has soaked, simmer for 20 minutes. Strain any remaining liquid, reserving the zest, into a measuring cup and add water to make 6 fl oz/175 ml/ ³/₄ cup.

3 Using a sharp knife, remove the peel from the oranges, discarding all the white pith. Cut the flesh widthwise into ¹/₄-inch/¹/₂-cm slices and arrange in a glass serving dish, scattered with a little of the orange zest. Reserve most of the zest to decorate.

4 Put the measured water and the sugar in a pan and heat until the sugar has dissolved, then bring to a boil and boil rapidly until it turns a pale golden color. Immediately remove from the heat, stir in the honey until dissolved. Let cool slightly, then pour the caramel sauce over the oranges. Chill in the refrigerator for at least 3 hours before serving, decorated with the reserved zest.